RESTAURANT REDEFINED

RESTAURANT REDEFINED

EXPLORING TRENDS IN THE RESTAURANT INDUSTRY

SAAMIA BUKHARI

NEW DEGREE PRESS

COPYRIGHT © 2020 SAAMIA BUKHARI

RESTAURANT REDEFINED

Exploring Trends in the Restaurant Industry

ISBN

978-1-64137-977-9   *Paperback*
978-1-64137-859-8   *Kindle Ebook*
978-1-64137-860-4   *Digital Ebook*

To my ever-loving parents.

CONTENTS

*Change is inevitable—except
from a vending machine.*

—ROBERT C. GALLAGHER

INTRODUCTION

———

Cambridge, Massachusetts. Home to Harvard University, the oldest surviving weekly newspaper in the United States, and the founding of Polaroid. But this city doesn't just boast a deep archive of history, art, and academia; it is accompanied by a rich, diverse cosmos of restaurants and food choices. And somewhere in that cosmos is one small, brilliant star—a small ramen joint called Yume Wo Katare.

Yume Wo Katare is not your average ramen restaurant. It's founded on a unique philosophy: if you can finish one of their generously massive bowls of Jiro-style ramen (thick noodles in a fatty, flavorful broth), you can accomplish anything.[1] Even if you're not able to finish your portion completely, the effort you put in that should be applied to all your endeavors in life. Quite inspiring, if you ask me.

———

[1] Herrine Ro and Luke Hansen, "Why people wait for hours to eat at this tiny Boston ramen workshop," Insider, Insider Inc., September 11, 2019.

After finishing a bowl of ramen, customers are encouraged to share a short-term and long-term goal out loud.[2] As unusual as it is, there's something special about announcing a dream you have to a room packed with complete strangers leading their own complex lives. And it's not as intimidating as you'd think.

Harvard Crimson contributor Amelia F. Roth-Dishy shares that "though the prospect may seem daunting, the employees are so charmingly laid-back that even the most timid public speaker would feel comfortable pronouncing their desires."[3] The atmosphere is warm, welcoming, and encouraging, with staff and customers cheering each other on. Yume Wo Katare urges customers to follow their dreams with a sense of perseverance, passion, and concentration, the same skills it takes to consume a massive portion of ramen diligently.

At the end of the meal, customers are also verbally scored on their consumption: "perfect," "good job," "almost," or "next time." Customers who finish the bowl in its entirety are awarded with "perfect!" while finishing noodles but not the broth earns a "good job!" and those not able to finish the challenge completely earn an "almost" or "next time."[4] Imagine being scored on your ability to finish a large bowl of ramen—definitely a new experience.

---

2   Kylie Obermeier, "Nightlife: Yume Wo Katare," BU Today, Boston University, February 11, 2016

3   Amelia F. Roth-Dishy, "Community Ramen Hotspot Still the Stuff of Dreams," *The Harvard Crimson*, October 30, 2018.

4   Andrea Shea, "Porter Square Ramen Shop Wants To Make Your Dreams Come True," WBUR, WBUR, July 16, 2014.

Yume Wo Katare, otherwise known as a "dream workshop," hopes to encourage customers to eat (and dream) beyond their self-imposed limits. This interactive experience separates Yume Wo Katare from other competing ramen locations, boasting a long waiting line, plenty of publicity, and enough word-of-mouth recommendations to keep it in business since owner Tsuyoshi Nishioka opened it up in 2012.[5]

Why bring up Yume Wo Katare? It perfectly exemplifies experiential dining, a necessity when competing with a flood of other restaurants in the area. Its philosophy, interactive element, and warm atmosphere are differentiating factors. After all, in a hypercompetitive environment, having great menu items is only one part of a successful restaurant establishment.

In the spring of 2018, about 660,755 restaurant units existed in the United States.[6] Fast forward to today: there are over one million restaurants operating in the United States as of 2019.[7] But just because more locations are opening does not mean that more of them are here to stay. In fact, a Cornell University study found that about 30 percent of restaurants go out of business in their first year of opening.[8] With more restaurants opening and the likelihood of going under raising uncertainty, what can restaurants do to stay afloat?

---

5   Kylie Obermeier, "Nightlife: Yume Wo Katare," BU Today, Boston University, February 11, 2016.

6   A. Elizabeth Sloan, "It's Time for Restaurant Realignment," *Food Technology Magazine* 72, no. 10 (October 2018).

7   "National Statistics," National Restaurant Association, accessed June 1, 2020.

8   H.G. Parsa, John T. Self, David Njite, and Tiffany King, "Why Restaurants Fail," Cornell Hotel and Restaurant Administration Quarterly 46, no. 3 (August 2005).

Constantly analyze and monitor the state of the industry. Deloitte's 2019 "Future of Food" report notes that "as a result of changing technology, consumer preferences, globalisation and demographics, the industry is evolving. The food ecosystem is becoming more complex and more interdependent. This is driven by consumers, whose spending on food, and food decisions, are shifting." [9] If the industry is changing, compromising both new and old establishments alike, what does that mean for the future?

Adaptation in response to the inevitable evolution. While there are many areas of the industry to explore, like employee demographics and wages, this book focuses on five broad areas in the context of customers. As Deloitte discusses, customers are responsible for major shifts in the industry, so these trends are in light of customer experience, interaction, and impact. In other words, this book is *not* exhaustive of every single trend in the restaurant industry from every angle under the sun. By the time that book came out, new trends would probably have taken hold! In *Restaurant Redefined*, we'll look into customer-centered trends that are tangible and impactful for the everyday, restaurant-intrigued reader.

Here are a few sneak peeks:

Technology: Kiosks! Tablets! Online ordering! There's no escaping technology in today's fast-paced world.

Marketing: Marketing is complex, and often interconnected with technology, like social media, digital strategy, loyalty

---

9   Adele Labine-Romain et al., "Future of Food," Deloitte, Deloitte Touche Tohmatsu, 2019.

programs—an abundance of tools to get customers through the door.

Sustainability: Restaurants are increasingly going local and being resourceful with food. Caring more matters and makes an impact on customers, the community, and the environment.

Food choice: How can restaurants decide their menu offerings? Ensure a menu as flavorful as it is profitable? Account for shifts in customer preferences? Look no further.

Experiential dining: What are differential factors? For example, in Yume Wo Katare's case, an interactive activity converts ramen into something more than a meal. It is a memorable, uplifting, and even personal experience.

These trends are not fads that will lose value in the near future. Restaurants are evolving in virtually every aspect. The dining experience will look different in the coming decades than it does today. Restaurants are no longer just sit-down establishments that bring the bill to you. They can take many forms and cater to more people than ever before (no pun intended). The question is, which establishments will adapt and which will be left behind?

* * *

I previously researched for a small private equity firm that sought to invest in local and regional food and beverage institutions doing well. I was surprised that both small and large restaurants have great capacity to thrive despite the challenges that come with today's landscape. It was also interesting to find that strong performance at one point does not guarantee success for the long term. Popular restaurants closed a few years after opening. All these variables highlight that what makes a "successful" restaurant is complex. That's why this book isn't supposed to dictate what makes a successful restaurant. There isn't a secret formula or code. The book peers into an important facet of what *can* contribute to a well-performing restaurant if adopted intelligently. I seek to explore today's restaurant trends in greater depth with research, a variety of interviews, and plenty of real-life examples—a great starting point for the curious customers of the world.

Dive into this book if you're interested in exploring intersections of food and technology, movement toward sustainability, and what makes the Starbucks's loyalty program so brilliant. Are you hungry for critical knowledge on industry trends? Then understand that adapting is imperative in a world of change. A changing restaurant outlook means operating as per usual will only work for so long. "The Restaurant of the Future" report by Deloitte asserts that "the restaurant industry is transforming and competition is more intense than ever before. 'Winning' restaurant brands will be those that best understand their customers, capitalize on digital technology options and analytics, and seize upon the opportunity to engage customers in a highly personalized way."[10] Trends for the future are taking shape now. If restaurants want to secure themselves, being cognizant of

---

10   Andrew Feinberg et al., "The Restaurant of the Future," Deloitte, Deloitte Development LLC., 2016.

trends and taking action (within appropriate means and context) is absolutely essential.

Get your forks and knives ready. There's a lot to digest.

CONTEXT

CHAPTER 1

BACKGROUND

When I first moved to Massachusetts, what shocked me the most was the tragic absence of Krispy Kreme Doughnuts stores. Though Krispy Kreme is a popular doughnut chain, you won't find it in every state. It was no longer a block or town away, no longer an immediately accessible option if my heart desired a chocolate-iced, glazed doughnut with sprinkles (my go-to). As an enthusiastic fan, the reality was appalling. But doughnut worry! For retail locations are here. Krispy Kreme supplies their doughnuts in grocery stores to reach customers they would otherwise not have access to. While hot, freshly made doughnuts are always superior, it is comforting to know I can still find the chain's glorious glazed delights in the aisles of a supermarket.

Chains like Krispy Kreme Doughnuts and White Castle constantly seek to reach new customers and grow. When White Castle first launched in 1921, it was home to famous five-cent hamburgers known as Sliders.[11] White Castle quickly made a name for itself as the world's first fast-food hamburger

---

11   "Our Story," White Castle Management Co., accessed June 1, 2020.

chain, selling bundles of Sliders in highly popular "Sacks."[12] The Kansas-born chain expanded its operations, now selling frozen Sliders in retail locations and offering online ordering options. White Castle is not alone in pushing out its products across the nation. Just check out prominent grocery stores: you'll see all sorts of restaurant products packaged for the everyday consumer, be it P.F. Chang's sesame sauce or IHOP breakfast sandwiches.

Restaurant trends have evolved over time. The twentieth century introduced chains like White Castle and McDonald's that helped establish the framework for the restaurant scene in the United States. Chains impacted the industry in many ways, including its size and its trends. The United States Department of Agriculture (USDA) emphasizes that "the expansion in numbers of restaurants in the latter half of the 20th century owed a great deal to the rise of chain restaurants" that were "linked by duplication of structure, theme, food, service, and amenities."[13] The chain and franchise model rapidly increased restaurant units and in turn led to more choices and competition. It also set fire to trends of convenience and accessibility that still persist today.

---

12 Ibid.

13 U.S. Department of Agriculture, Economic Research Service, *America's Eating Habits: Food Away From Home,* by Michelle J. Saksena, Abigail M. Okrent, Tobenna D. Anekwe, Clare Cho, Christopher Dicken, Anne Effland, Howard Elitzak, Joanne Guthrie, Karen S. Hamrick, Jeffrey Hyman, Young Jo, Biing-Hwan Lin, Lisa Mancino, Patrick W. McLaughlin, Ilya Rahkovsky, Katherine Ralston, Travis A. Smith, Hayden Stewart, Jessica Todd, and Charlotte Tuttle, (September 2018).

McDonald's pounced on the idea of convenience by launching its Speedee Service System in 1948.[14] The Speedee Service System, as its name suggests, allowed for more efficient operations. Its core elements included cheap prices, standardized orders, and minimized menus.[15] "What Henry Ford had done for cars, the McDonald brothers did for hamburgers and French fries: they broke down processes into simple, repetitive tasks" which allowed them to "churn out food quickly, cheaply and consistently. There was nothing else like it."[16] Streamlining completely transforming the business.

With contenders like White Castle and McDonald's, fast, convenient, and cheap options were the rage for working– and middle-class families in the twentieth century. By the 1990s, more people started eating out as family households changed.[17] No longer was there only one breadwinner in the family. With two streams of income, middle-class Americans could afford to go to restaurants more often. In response to a shift in consumption, restaurants tailored their offerings. Adapting to new patterns, "restaurant chains like Olive Garden, Applebee's, and 99 catered to the ever-growing middle class, offering moderately priced meals and children's menus."[18]

---

14   Hadley Meares, "The Real McDonald's: The San Bernardino Origins of a Fast Food Empire," KCET, Public Media Group of Southern California, August 5, 2016.

15   Ibid.

16   Tim Harford, "How McDonald's revolutionised business," *BBC*, February 5, 2020.

17   Lorri Mealy, "A History of the Restaurant," The Balance Small Business, Dotdash, December 13, 2018.

18   Ibid.

As mentioned earlier, an increasing number of restaurants entered the scene over time, flooding the market. This introduces a problem today, since "there are simply too many places to eat," says Victor Fernandez, executive director of hospitality data firm Black Box Intelligence.[19] The issue is that "half of our food dollar is now going to restaurants, but we have more supply than we have demand," Fernandez reveals.[20] With competition fierce, what can restaurants do? Analyze and tailor their services to trends, as we will discuss in further detail soon.

Where water goes, life will follow. Similarly, as customer patterns shift over time, restaurants also change. It's only natural. From large chains like Burger King experimenting with plant-based options to small businesses using in-house technology, each does what it can to survive in the future. Today, restaurants sink or swim in the turbulent waters of the industry. Staying afloat is possible with the help of a life jacket: adapting over time.

---

19   Derek Thompson, "The Paradox of American Restaurants," *The Atlantic*, June 20, 2017.

20   Ibid.

CHAPTER 2

CURRENT STATUS

———

"There are three things that will never go out of business: doctors, diapers, and food," my uncle Tariq once told me jokingly at a family get-together. While it is founded on obviously oversimplified logic, his comment does bear an element of truth when it comes to food. Food is always going to be important. Looking at food in the context of the restaurant industry and its expected growth, business is *booming*, at least for the next decade. As for his assertion about doctors and diapers, well, that's a whole different book.

What is the current status of the industry? First of all, the restaurant industry is huge, with over one million locations in the United States as of 2019.[21] But what's even more shocking is its projected growth. The National Restaurant Association reveals that sales are expected to reach $1.2 *trillion* by 2030.[22] What's interesting is that for 2019, sales for 2020 were projected

---

21   "National Statistics," National Restaurant Association, accessed June 1, 2020.

22   "National Restaurant Association Unveils its Restaurant Industry 2030 Report," National Restaurant Association, November 5, 2019.

to hit $899 billion.[23] Over the span of a decade, projected sales are expected to increase by $301 billion. *301 billion.*

What fuels this high growth? A variety of factors. Shifts to off-premises, increased attention on sustainability, changing labor force demographics, and technology are all some major key players in understanding the current and predicted status of the restaurant industry.[24] Knowing this foundation is helpful to better understanding specific trends discussed in this book.

One factor is the changing definition of a restaurant thanks to growth of off-premise options. "Off-premise" refers to adding value outside a physical or traditional restaurant space, such as "delivery, virtual restaurants, subscription services, and grab-and-go at retail locations."[25] Think Uber Eats or a restaurant's own delivery system, for example. Customers do not need to go into the physical restaurant location to gain the benefits of the service, making it "off-premises."

It's now easier than ever to have a meal delivered (example of "off-premises"), especially since online delivery (covered later in the book) is accessible and growing. That means it will take more effort to keep the average customer interested in going to a restaurant in person, otherwise referred to as "on-premises." Faster, easier, and more accessible off-premises alternatives are out there as competition.

---

23   "National Statistics," National Restaurant Association, accessed June 1, 2020.

24   "National Restaurant Association Unveils its Restaurant Industry 2030 Report," National Restaurant Association, November 5, 2019.

25   Ibid.

I'm no stranger to the benefits of off-premises options as a customer. When I was a freshman at the University of Illinois at Urbana-Champaign (before I transferred to Boston College), I sometimes ordered Domino's Pizza to my dorm on chilly nights (Illinois weather is no joke), illustrating my preference for off-premises options in that circumstance. I wouldn't dare go to a restaurant in biting weather. Plus, you can only eat dining hall food for so long!

But what does it mean for restaurants to "do more" to drive foot traffic? With shifting attitudes toward "on-premises," one way to spark interest is through experiential dining.[26] Experiential dining focuses on the entire customer experience, asking questions including "What role does service play?" "Are wait times justifiable?" and "Is there something unique and special about being there in person?" And that's just the beginning.

You might ask why it is important to consider every facet of the customer experience. Deloitte highlights that "for restaurants in this competitive, fast-moving space, differentiating on these new and evolving experiential elements will likely separate the winners from the losers."[27] As discussed in the introduction, Yume Wo Katare exemplifies experiential dining perfectly with its dream-centered activities and warm community. You'll read more about this critical factor later in the book.

---

26   Ibid.

27   Ashley Reichheld et al., "Through guests' eyes," Deloitte, Deloitte Development LLC., 2017.

Another reason for this sharp rise in expected sales stems from the increased importance of sustainability and nutrition.[28] Restaurants can address sustainability and nutrition with food options, preparation, overall supply chain, and more. Customers are paying more attention to how food found its way to their table and food choices. In fact, a 2018 Food and Health survey found that knowing where food comes from and that it contains natural ingredients are two important factors in restaurant selection for customers.[29] This funnels into the report's assertion that "restaurants will need to adapt to evolving dietary restrictions and consumer preferences" to stay competitive.[30] This evolution includes the rise of veganism, keto, paleo, and raw food diets, the rise of food allergies requiring innovation including allergies to dairy, eggs, and wheat, halal and kosher alternatives, and more.

While not covered in this book, the changing labor force also contributes to the current status. Though areas of technology in the space will rapidly take hold, labor force goes in the opposite direction. Between 2018 and 2028, there is projected to be a slow labor-rate (.5 percent annually), with an increase in adults in the labor force hitting 16.1 million people by 2028, paired with a 5.1 million decrease in teenagers in the labor force by the same years.[31] Demographics are changing,

---

28 "National Restaurant Association Unveils its Restaurant Industry 2030 Report," National Restaurant Association, November 5, 2019.

29 "2018 Food and Health Survey," International Food Information Council Foundation, 2018.

30 "National Restaurant Association Unveils its Restaurant Industry 2030 Report," National Restaurant Association, November 5, 2019.

31 Ibid.

meaning restaurants will place more emphasis on recruiting and acquiring older talent.

McDonald's is already taking action to recruit older employees by collaborating with the US interest group American Association of Retired Persons (AARP). "In addition to posting its jobs on the AARP Job Board, McDonald's also is working with AARP... to start a pilot program to help older adults return to work after they have been out of the workforce."[32] This is just one example of how restaurants must devise new strategies to satisfy their employment needs.

Changing demographics mean "operators will automate more routine back-of-house tasks to enhance productivity and efficiency," incorporating technology to the shift.[33] For example, the implementation of kiosks in the physical restaurant space totally changes the game. It lowers labor costs, cuts down on customer wait time, and changes the overall dining experience. While automation can complete a variety of tasks like flipping burgers or scanning labels, sometimes the automation itself can be the experience, whether it be back-of-house or in interaction with the customers, as we will explore in a chapter coming soon.

One example is Spyce, an automated restaurant in Boston that dishes out flavorful, affordable, and nutritious bowls.[34] Once a customer places an order via kiosk, meals are cooked by

---

32 Kenneth Terrell, "McDonald's and AARP Team Up to Fill Jobs,"
    AARP, April 25, 2019.

33 "National Restaurant Association Unveils its Restaurant Industry 2030
    Report," National Restaurant Association, November 5, 2019.

34 "Who We Are," Spyce, Spyce Food Co., accessed June 1, 2020.

"constantly tumbling the food" in rotating pans heated with induction and temperature controls to "perfectly cook your meal every time."[35] Themes of technology and experiential dining intersect to illustrate a competitive restaurant in the fast-casual landscape.

A variety of factors contribute to the expected growth of the industry—off-premises options, customer preferences, demographics, technology, and more—highlighting its sheer complexity. But that shouldn't stop restaurants from acting. It is up to restaurants to take heed of what is driving industry growth and tailor it to best suit their own operations. Staying on top of trend history, current status, and need to adapt is helpful for businesses to make informed decisions going forward.

---

35 *Spycefoodco*, "Spyce - Robotic Restaurant by Four MIT Graduates in Collaboration with Chef Daniel Boulud," May 3, 2018, video, 2:29.

CHAPTER 3

ADAPTING INTELLIGENTLY

When I lived in the South, my family and I decided to check out a peculiar restaurant after stumbling on a good coupon. When we visit relatively unknown establishments, it can go two ways. One, it's a hidden gem we enjoy and revisit a lot while in the area. Or two, it's a place we were better off not trying out thanks to subpar food, service, or experience—memorable, but not in a good way. Unfortunately, this one falls in the latter category.

We didn't know what to expect, since the outside of the restaurant was plastered with a variety of fonts and arrows. We soon discovered that it was costume-themed, with servers dressing up as a range of fictional and real-life people from Snow White to Elvis Presley. The physical layout was a series of nooks for each table, each with a different theme. Colorful wood beams held up the restaurant, in which furniture from all eras filled the space. No two tables had the same types of chairs. Random banners and flags hung from the ceiling. I counted over a dozen different light fixtures. It was definitely different. And sensory overload. Only by reading the menu could I get a sense of what the establishment served: standard American food.

By trying to do everything, in a way, the restaurant accomplished nothing. Without having a clear direction of what it stands for, it was simply a blur of colors. To be competitive does not mean to be the most out there, the most different, or the most unique. As customers, it was difficult to grasp what the identity of the restaurant was, since there was a conflict with atmosphere, menu, and expectations—too much of *everything* to be anything. If a restaurant is not clear about this, it struggles to not only share its vision with customers but also adapt over time while still being true to its roots.

Adapting sounds simple, but it's rather complicated. It's not just about catering to changing customer preferences or industry trends. It's about integrating that change in the business itself, so it fits with the organization of the restaurant.

A KPMG report asserts that "preferences for healthier food options, concerns over environmental sustainability, increased competition from grocery stores, heightened consumer expectations, and rapidly advancing technology are reinventing the traditional dining experience and forcing change on how the industry operates."[36] The word "forced" is the key word. Business as usual is no longer a sustainable

---

36   Paul Fultz, Joel Rampoldt, and Dan Shaughnessy, "An Appetite for Change," KPMG, KPMG LLP, 2016.

option. However, it is not easy for businesses to enact change if the industry itself does not invite it.

The report offers two steps to the industry to be open to change:

The first is challenging the status quo. People fear that doing so is risky. This is true. Restaurants default to traditionality since it "tends to reward well-executed, low-risk change," something that will only be true for so long.[37] Celebrating failure through risk would encourage more action. Disruptive action may be a shock to an industry that has been resistant to change but in fact has great potential for success.

The second is integrating innovation. If change is intertwined with operations, restaurants can adapt meaningfully. An important point to remember is that "there is no single answer to innovating successfully, no one-size-fits-all solution" in establishing a "framework for innovation."[38] Therefore, different ideas for innovation and adaptation are all relative. There is not a secret recipe for success. Customization to the restaurant's identity, operations, and more is key.

The trends outlined in this book and beyond must be considered intelligently. Similar to the restaurant I mentioned at the beginning of the chapter, by trying to do everything without clear direction, the customer is lost on the journey. It's not about catering to every single trend that makes a strong restaurant. That's not the point. The point is to understand the trends and apply what fits with the overall fit of the

---

37   Ibid.

38   Ibid.

restaurant. It's not a cookie-cutter type of deal. Restaurants are advised to consider trends in light of themselves. How can it be applied, customized, and make sense at an individual level? Finding that "sweet spot" is a personal and complex journey but one for restaurants to think about to truly adapt in a personal, integrative way.

TECHNOLOGY

CHAPTER 4

ONLINE ORDERING

When was the last time you ordered food from your favorite restaurant?

I was hanging out with my college friends Hannah and Lana for a movie night. Engrossed in playing competitive card games (we go on for hours) at Lana's apartment, it was only past 10 p.m. that we decided to finally put on the movie. However, it was too late to grab ingredients from our local grocery store to make a home-cooked meal to accompany our film. And of course, you can't watch a movie on an empty stomach. That's when the convenience of food delivery came to play, since many locations deliver well through the night. Plus, in an area packed with college students, online ordering is especially in demand.

Lana pulled out her phone and scrolled through different online food delivery options, as Hannah and I pondered on what to choose (it's an important decision). The options to consider were endless. Classic cheese pizza from a big chain? Chicken tacos from a nearby Mexican restaurant? Lana introduced me to a local Chinese restaurant I had never heard of before, convincing Hannah and I to try it out. Why not? We placed an order through the restaurant's delivery app. Easy. Within twenty minutes, our food came, piping hot. It was perfect because we could satisfy our late-night hunger in comfort. There's nothing like warm, freshly pulled noodles with a side of tea while watching a horror movie with your closest friends.

* * *

Let's take this individual case of online food delivery and apply it to the national level for context. Forty-four percent of consumers report that they have placed an order using a restaurant app or website in the past year.[39] People are familiar with the process. But that's only looking at restaurant-specific apps and websites. What about third-party platforms like Uber Eats? A US Foods survey reveals that "the average person has two delivery apps and uses them three times a month."[40] A competitive need for restaurants to offer online ordering.

We've looked at online ordering's prevalence when it comes to the average customer. How long will the trend persist? Sarwant Singh, senior partner at marketing research firm Frost & Sullivan, predicts that online ordering will experience explosive growth. Singh asserts that "online food delivery is set to supersize to a hefty $200 billion by 2025."[41]

---

39   "2019 Restaurant Industry Factbook," National Restaurant Association, accessed June 1, 2020.

40   "New Study Shows What Consumers Crave in a Food Delivery Service," US Foods, US Foods Inc., 2019.

41   Sarwant Singh, "The Soon To Be $200B Online Food Delivery Is Rapidly Changing The Global Food Industry," Forbes, Forbes Media

It's not only Singh who presses the gravity and potential of online delivery, however. A June 2018 UBS Investment Bank report estimates that "the global online food ordering market could grow more than tenfold over the next decade or so, to \$365bn by 2030 from \$35bn today."[42] \$365 billion by 2030 shows that online food delivery is not going anywhere anytime soon.

I had the opportunity to gain greater insight on online delivery from Patrick O'Reilly, a principal at Marcum LLP who consults his clients on innovative technological and accounting solutions. He also is a publican at his restaurant, O'Reilly's Cure Restaurant & Bar in Scarborough, Maine.

O'Reilly shared that it is important for growth-oriented restaurants to expand their operations with technology, like providing options of online ordering. Relying solely on "in-house computers isn't necessarily scalable, affordable, or portable to the web," he said. This serves as a competitive disadvantage to other restaurants "that can be nimble and scale up" quickly, O'Reilly pointed out. Therefore, he noted that a number of food and beverage institutions make the "pivot from just in-house sale to takeout, pickup, delivery" to give customers more choices.

Some ways restaurants take advantage of the growing trend of online ordering is through their own system or partnering with a third-party platform like DoorDash, Uber Eats, Grubhub or

---

LLC., September 9, 2019.

42 "Is the Kitchen Dead?" UBS Investment Bank, UBS Securities, June 18, 2018.

Postmates. Like many customers, I never really paid attention to how I ordered food online. But after talking to O'Reilly and researching more, I learned that the method of ordering matters immensely to a restaurant, from exposure to control.

O'Reilly illustrated the financial savings of using a restaurant's own ordering system over a third-party platform with a hamburger example. Imagine you owned a restaurant, selling a gourmet hamburger for $11. Using your own web-based portal, "you can have that order, processed efficiently without a whole lot of human interaction and sell it for eleven dollars." What was listed on the menu, you earn—$11 processed smoothly. Boom.

On the other hand, say you opted for a third-party platform. This shakes things up. Now you have to account for fees that the platform charges you. In turn, you would have to "change the price of that burger to say, $14 or $15 to get you back to the same exact profit margin." Are the fees so costly that you have to hike up your prices that high to compensate? Yes. Uber Eats, DoorDash, and other third-party platforms charge "roughly 30 percent" in fees, which O'Reilly shared is a "significant haircut on margins" for a restaurant.

Before I learned about fees, I questioned why a sandwich ordered from Uber Eats could be priced higher than actually buying the sandwich from the restaurant in-person. Learning that restaurants charge more to compensate for fees informs why restaurants price items the way they do.

High fees are not the only reason restaurant owners may avoid third-party online ordering platforms. O'Reilly brought up that restaurants would lose "some control over the quality of that meal being delivered to the customer" since there is "another party involved in the transaction, not only financially but physically to facilitate the delivery." The middleman (third-party platform) takes the reins on the delivery now. Singh echoes O'Reilly's thoughts. In partnering with third-party platforms, Singh mentions that it is important for restaurants to recognize risks and "high rates of cash burn" associated with it, including the fact that "logistical reliability and product quality are beyond their control."[43]

In what ways do restaurants lose control when opting for a third-party platform? O'Reilly mentioned a variety of examples, including the "driver may or may not give preference to your customer or your restaurant when they're picking up that delivery," not being able to ensure that the food is "hot and fresh," or not guaranteeing friendly service during the delivery process. All these experiences affect the customer at the end, as well as the customer's perception. Therefore, "if a customer is unhappy with either [logistical reliability and product quality], the online food company has to bear the monetary penalty," Singh said.[44] In addition to (literally) paying the price when it comes to potential costs of third-party delivery, Singh also discusses issues of fraud, including "restaurant manipulated 'ghost' deliveries or cybersecurity loopholes related to digital payments" that prevent restaurants from remaining competitive in the space.

---

43   Sarwant Singh, "The Soon To Be $200B Online Food Delivery Is Rapidly Changing The Global Food Industry," Forbes, Forbes Media LLC., September 9, 2019.

44   Ibid.

One example is the case against Grubhub. In 2019, "a number of restaurant owners [had] joined a class action lawsuit against Grubhub, alleging the service is sneakily charging restaurants up to hundreds of dollars more a month," like "counting non-order calls as orders, and charging restaurants for things like customer questions or complaints."[45] Yikes. While a Grubhub spokesperson finds the lawsuit to be "without merit," it does probe further inquiry on the detriments and delivery issues of third-party platforms, since high fees put restaurants in a tight position to begin with.[46]

With all the negatives associated with third-party platforms, why do so many restaurants, big and small, use them? O'Reilly explained that if restaurants do not have a "good alternative" like a point-of-sale system to conduct the operation themselves, then it makes sense to use such platforms. Others may find the process to be "cumbersome, difficult, or expensive," so third-party platforms are often "their only option." This is particularly common with smaller businesses that use pen and paper and traditional cash registers to take down orders. It is more convenient to use Uber Eats or DoorDash versus spending money on a whole new system, changing the entire transaction process of a restaurant.

In addition, third-party platforms give restaurants exposure to a massive, hungry user base that an individual restaurant platform would not have access to. For example, Grubhub boasts over twenty-four million "active diners," and "features over 300,000 restaurants," uncovering just how much opportunity

---

45   Jaya Saxena, "Delivery Apps Aren't Getting Any Better," Eater, Vox Media, LLC., May 29, 2019.

46   Ibid.

there is to attract new customers.[47] Twenty-four million active diners almost equals Australia's population. Wild. Uber Eats, Grubhub, DoorDash, and Postmates are the most popular apps among consumers, thanks to easy usage and a tailored experience.[48] Tapping into where the customers are, restaurants can cast a wide net and fish out new customers.

Considering its immense growth in the coming years, online ordering shows significant promise for restaurants. Even if they may not direct control of every part of the delivery process and are subject to paying high fees, there are merits. The ease, exposure, and customer accessibility restaurants gain from third-party platforms are unparalleled. Restaurants must decide what online ordering platform and strategy is best suited for their business.

* * *

One interesting nugget of information is that not all online orders are derived from a traditional restaurant itself. Ghost kitchens are on the rise, otherwise known as cloud kitchens or virtual kitchens. Sounds futuristic, but it's more common than you'd think, at least in bustling, high-density areas. "Commercial spaces that were once restaurants open as ghost kitchens" and are "going to become more and more evident," O'Reilly explained. He shared that while living in New York City for ten years, "there were places you could order takeout from," but "you could never go there" in person. Does it sound

---

47   "About Us," Grubhub, accessed June 1, 2020.

48   "New Study Shows What Consumers Crave in a Food Delivery Service," US Foods, US Foods Inc., 2019.

ominous? Well, ghost *is* in the name. "There is just a street address on the door," O'Reilly said, describing the typical New York ghost kitchen environment. All takeout—and it has been that way "even back in the eighties," O'Reilly added.

O'Reilly discussed that what makes ghost kitchens increasingly popular are the savings and efficiency. Ghost kitchens can be efficient on the "food side alone without those additional costs and a much smaller footprint in terms of the lease." Because it is all takeout, ghost kitchens do not need to worry about servers, glassware, furniture, and other expenses, investments, or costs. They are simply kitchens to prepare meals for delivery. That lets ghost kitchens keep more money in their pockets than dishing it out to sustain a pristine dining environment and hiring people to keep it running. You won't find ghost kitchens everywhere, though. The trend of online ordering from ghost kitchens is seen "particularly in high-density urban areas" like New York City. O'Reilly emphasized that it's not going to just continue but also increase as it "squeezes out traditional dining service." Ghost kitchens aren't ghosting customers anytime soon.

* * *

Technology is woven in many aspects of our everyday lives, from navigating a new city with a map on our phones to home security systems. It is inevitable for it to be applied to the restaurant industry in a multitude of ways. By embracing and maximizing different forms of technology, restaurants can stay current and competitive. Considering the strong growth rate for online food delivery in the future, offering online ordering is essential for business. Time to think outside the (takeout) box.

CHAPTER 5

IN-HOUSE

As of June 2019, McDonald's has been experimenting with voice-activated drive-throughs to reduce wait time and ensure smooth service.[49] There have been a range of performances thus far, from customers who receive their order quickly and correctly to an instance when "a worker had to step in for one customer who hesitated during his order, tripping up the software."[50] While still in the test phase, McDonald's investment makes clear that restaurants, at least those with the time and capital to invest, are not afraid to try new types of technology in an effort to learn how to improve business. By incorporating technology, restaurants are able to improve ordering, payment, and overall efficiency more than ever. Voice and bot technology, food waste, and adding value to the customer are emerging categories in restaurant technology, funneling into in-house operations.[51]

---

49 Heather Haddon, "McDonald's Tests Robot Fryers and Voice-Activated Drive-Throughs," *The Wall Street Journal*, June 20, 2019.

50 Ibid.

51 Brita Rosenheim, "The Future of Restaurant Tech: Serving the Next Course," Forbes, Forbes Media LLC., November 11, 2019.

VOICE AND BOT TECHNOLOGY

Voice and bot technology has been implemented in a variety of other industries, such as in phone calls and for Siri and Alexa. Now it is just beginning to create impact in the restaurant industry, though its role has room to grow. This technology can be seen with drive-throughs or phone ordering to understand and process orders effectively, typically fit for chains like Chipotle Mexican Grill.

Chipotle has been experimenting with voice artificial intelligence—not in drive-throughs like McDonald's, but in their phone orders since early 2018. Nation's Restaurant News noted that Chipotle's "10-unit test grew to 1,800 locations this year."[52] On top of that, Nicole West, Chipotle's vice president of digital strategy and product, shared that "the 2,500-unit chain plans to expand the AI voice system to its remaining US stores by the end of the year."[53] When a customer dials to order, a female voice listens to the customer's order and offers suggestions.

"With each transaction, she learns the idiosyncrasies of how people order. She might stumble if someone responds "combo" when requesting a mix of pinto and black beans. But once she figures it out, her algorithm remembers," Nation's Restaurant News explained. Therefore, the more orders, the more learning, West emphasizes.[54] Chipotle is still in the process of determining the efficacy of the technology considering it is in its early stages, though the main goal is to improve the

---

52   Nancy Luna, "Chipotle Mexican Grill quietly rolls out voice AI to 1,800 units," Nation's Restaurant News, Informa USA, Inc., July 20, 2019.

53   Ibid.

54   Ibid.

customer experience. While voice and bot technology is in the experimental phase at large, it is indeed an emerging and intriguing category of technology in the industry that larger chains have the money to test.

FOOD WASTE

As of 2016, France prohibits grocery stores from discarding food that can still be eaten, instead directing them to donate the unsold items to charities. While France has a food-waste law, for other countries, individuals are responsible for minimizing waste, be they chefs, restaurant owners, or customers.[55] For some restaurant owners, saving money and minimizing waste can go hand in hand, especially with in-house technology. Waste ranges from leftover waste in the kitchen to customer leftovers to the supply chain itself. One way to combat this issue is by tracking inventory through a point-of-sale system, detailed later in this chapter, and also monitoring which menu items are selling and which are not, to make strategic decisions. If this interests you, keep reading! More information on food waste is covered in in the "Sustainability" section of this book.

DELIVER VALUE

Another trend to keep an eye out for is how restaurants can best deliver value to the customer with technology.[56] Quite

---

55 Melanie Saltzman, Christopher Livesay, Joan Martelli, and Deborah Gouffran, "Is France's groundbreaking food-waste law working?" PBS, NewsHour Productions LLC., August 21, 2019.

56 Brita Rosenheim, "The Future of Restaurant Tech: Serving the Next Course," Forbes, Forbes Media LLC., November 11, 2019.

open-ended, delivering value can happen in numerous ways. It can range from using data to craft personalized food recommendations on mobile apps to using social media to market information to a certain demographic and keep them interested. Even loyalty programs can add value to the customer and create a meaningful connection, important when it comes to customer loyalty. All these ways to add value and more are explained in later chapters.

NFC TAGS

NFC tags are another technology gaining more traction. NFC is the acronym for near field communication, and at a high level, is a technology that allows NFC-enabled devices to communicate and share information with one another within a small radius.[57] If a person uses Apple Pay or Samsung Pay, for example, they will have to hold their device close to another NFC-enabled device to share that information, applicable for virtually any industry. The small radius is widely regarded as beneficial because it provides a security benefit when it comes to sensitive information with payment. NFC tags are helpful in restaurants for facilitating food orders from the table to the kitchen.

NFC technology has begun to be tested in several different restaurants, including Chick-fil-A.[58] Starting in October 2019, Chick-fil-A employed NFC technology-powered dine-in mobile ordering in participating locations. It works by the customer placing a "dine-in" order through the Chick-fil-A app, tapping

---

57 Simon Hill. "What is NCF? Here's everything you need to know," Digital Trends, Designtechnica Corporation, May 6, 2020.

58 Dan Berthiaume, "Chick-Fil-A eliminates lines with new mobile service," Chain Store Age, EnsembleIQ, October 17, 2019.

their device to a table number in the physical location, and an employee bringing the food to the tapped table once ready. Customers can place orders without having to leave their table or wait in line, having their food delivered straight to them.

Chick-fil-A's director of service and hospitality, Khalilah Cooper, affirms this benefit, stating that the "technology will be particularly helpful for busy parents who can now head straight into the restaurant and have their meal brought to their table at their convenience, without waiting in line."[59] But the support for this technology did not happen right away.

The chain decided to run with NFC after it ran a pilot in over eighty locations to gauge the effectiveness of the technology. Highlighting the high level of satisfaction found with the mobile ordering only possible with NFC tags, "internal Chick-fil-A research indicated that 92 percent of customers surveyed that used dine-in mobile ordering found the feature appealing due to ease and convenience."[60] Based on its success with customers, Chick-fil-A decided to move forward with it in select locations.

Cooper capitalizes on the importance of technology to grow Chick-fil-A. The director asserts that the chain is "focused on how the design of the physical restaurant environment can make the ordering and meal fulfillment journey even more seamless and enjoyable."[61] Making it as easy and convenient for the customer provides for a pleasant experience.

---

59   Ibid.

60   Ibid.

61   Jonathan Maze, "Chick-Fil-A Introduces Mobile Dine-In Ordering," Restaurant Business Online, Winsight LLC., October 17, 2019.

NFC tags are one of emerging applications of in-house uses of technology but not exactly the most widespread. Security and privacy risks, usability, usefulness, cost, and ability to be tested are factors restaurants must explore to evaluate if NFC technology is a good fit for a restaurant's goals.[62] After all, Chick-fil-A ran a pilot test to learn from customers before diving in and only at select locations. Kiosk and tablet transactions, however, are growing for small and large restaurants alike.

POS TECHNOLOGY

Peter Romeo of Restaurant Business noted that 84 percent of 279 executives of "food and beverage sellers that were using mobile technology" found that "their labor costs have been reduced by guest-facing mobile tech, and a similar majority (86 percent) attest that the digital devices have cut service times and boosted throughput."[63] Popular guest-facing technology includes self-order kiosks and integrated tablets. These devices fall under point-of-sale technology, or POS, which do more than just let a customer order a meal by tapping a screen. Point-of-sale hardware and software "enables a business to take orders, track sales, manage cash flow, and keep track of inventory across multiple locations."[64]

---

62 Vedat Coskun, Busra Ozdenizci, and Kerem Ok, "The Survey on Near Field Communication," Sensors, June 5, 2015.

63 Peter Romeo, "Restaurants Admit Strong Fears About Keeping up with Tech," Restaurant Business Online, Winsight LLC., April 23, 2019.

64 Keefer, Kaitlin, "5 Tech Solutions You Need to Grow Your Restaurant Business," SquareUp, Square, Inc., accessed June 1, 2020.

In addition, POS specialist Jason Feemster explained that "many types of restaurants need to utilize a POS like full-service restaurants, quick-service restaurants, fast food, take-out only, cafes, pizza shops, etc."[65] It is important to have POS systems in restaurants to accept different types of payments, manage inventory, track transactions, and send orders from the device straight to the kitchen, maximizing efficiency.

What's great about POS systems compared to the traditional cash register is that it provides an immense amount of data. Data is the new gold—extremely valuable. One can take this information to predict the future based on what the restaurant itself is experiencing in its day-to-day operations. The system has numerous benefits: you can monitor inventory based on sales of certain menu items to stock appropriately, decrease wait time with a more efficient ordering system, keep track of customer details to cater to their preferences, check reports to see performance over time to identify trends, limit errors, and be connected across different locations.[66] Owners can buy various add-ons to tailor the system to their business, like accounting and labor management solutions.

POS systems can be accessed on different platforms, from tablet to smartphone. Implementing this system when starting out may seem like overkill, so restaurants need to consider whether this is financially possible or not. The perk about having access to data when starting is that right off the bat one can keep track of statistics and work from there. Starting

---

65   Jason Feemster, "What is POS? The Definitive Definition and Guide," POS USA, May 21, 2020.

66   "Top 10 Benefits of a POS System" Dallas POS, February 15, 2020.

out with a traditional cash register may save a restaurant money but does so at the expense of analytics necessary to make strategic decisions.

Self-order kiosks are one example of POS technology that offer many benefits for customers, employees, and managers. A study by Tillster reported that "by 2024, the global kiosk market is expected to reach $30.8 billion, with a significant portion of that coming from food & beverage kiosks."[67] Bruce Rasmussen, director of strategic verticals for Ingenico Group, details eight benefits of eliminating the cash register and adopting a "kiosk strategy," including: shorter wait times, improved order accuracy, improved data collection, ease in joining loyalty programs, increased upselling of additional items, lower labor costs, acceptance of various payment methods, and an overall improvement in customer experience.[68]

Gunther Plosch, Wendy's chief financial officer, stated that "about two-thirds of our company restaurants" have kiosks and that "we are seeing benefits and are trying to convince the rest of the system to make the capital investment because we think it has a return," highlighting the technology's potential and at the same time, cost.[69]

I've experienced the ease and benefits of a self-ordering kiosk myself. On a busy day at Taco Bell, I went straight toward the

---

67 Ingenico Group, "Self-Service Kiosks Are Becoming More Popular in Restaurants," EVO, EVO Payments Inc., August 29, 2019.

68 Bruce Rasmussen, "8 reasons restaurants need a kiosk strategy," Fast Casual, Networld Media Group, LLC., July 12, 2018.

69 Alicia Kelso, "Self-Order Kiosks Are Finally Having A Moment In The Fast Food Space," Forbes, Forbes Media LLC., July 20, 2019.

self-serve kiosks to avoid waiting in line and simply order food in peace. Doing so also meant I was more prone to buying additional items featured (upselling) or ordering more knowing I was not pressured by external influences, like a blank stare of the cashier. Ultimately, consumer spending increases with kiosks as the trend continues to grow.

Another use of POS technology is through tablet systems, be it tabletop or handheld. This form is becoming increasingly popular when it comes to transactions, like Square, Toast, Lightspeed, ShopKeep, and Revel. The Paris Creperie in Brookline, Massachusetts implements this technology. I completed payment right through the tablet after the cashier logged in my order, emailing my receipt shortly after. My friends and I were able to order and sit down at a table quickly since the technology in place made it easy. One point for satisfaction right there. Plus, their chicken pesto crêpe was very good. One more point for fantastic food. Making customers happy with ease in ordering demonstrates how POS is beneficial for a variety of parties involved.

In-house technology covers a range of areas: voice and bot technology, food waste, delivering value, NFC, and POS technology. Attempting to implement all advancements in technology in the restaurant space is not the goal for restaurants.

As Deloitte's "Restaurant of the Future" describes:

> "Taken separately, each of these digital applications is impressive. But a restaurant brand that actually does treat them separately may end up managing a disjointed array of gimmicks instead

of a comprehensive service model. On the other hand, if a restaurant offers digital enhancements that are tightly coordinated and work in concert, it can take advantage of the data that comes out of them and deliver efficient, personalized customer experiences."[70]

Ultimately, a successful use of technology requires tailoring technology to a restaurant's own operations in an interconnected fashion.

---

70   Andrew Feinberg et al., "Restaurant of the Future," Deloitte, Deloitte Development LLC., 2016.

CHAPTER 6

AUTOMATION

___

Spyce is a fully automated fast-casual restaurant briefly mentioned at the beginning of the book. A customer first places an order on a tablet, and robots use induction-heating to cook their signature, creative "bowls" with speed and accuracy.[71] Since its opening in Boston in 2018, the fascinating food institution has attracted a variety of people: first, customers through piquing interest with a novel restaurant idea; second, tech investors who find value and potential in innovative automation; and third, chefs to help devise the menu and create new culinary creations for the available options, something a robot could never do.

What's interesting about Spyce is that it is not a huge, dominating chain using automation. Unlike Olive Garden using tablets at all of its locations thanks to its partnership with Ziosk, Spyce is much smaller yet still has potential for high growth, as technology is part of the experiential dining experience.[72]

---

71 *Spycefoodco*, "Spyce - Robotic Restaurant by Four MIT Graduates in Collaboration with Chef Daniel Boulud," May 3, 2018, video, 2:29.

72 Tracey Lien, "Olive Garden rolls out tabletop tablets for ordering and payment," *Los Angeles Times*, April 14, 2015.

In fact, the restaurant is looking to expand to Cambridge, Massachusetts and continuously works to improve its menu and technology.[73] For Spyce, technology has several roles, highlighting the breadth of automation: efficiency, proper cooking, accuracy of orders, and speed.

Automation also acts as unique factor that attracts customers in person, driving foot traffic with press, publicity, word-of-mouth recommendations, and more. I actually first heard about Spyce through my dad, since the restaurant's robotic aspect is an intriguing conversation starter. It is not every day you can watch a robot make delicious bowls of food with relatively low prices that cater to young people in the area. Automation serving tasty food is a critical point of differentiation that helps drive Spyce's success.

* * *

Online ordering and in-house technology are some forms of the greater trend of automation. In 2016, McKinsey & Company concluded that "73 percent of the activities workers perform in food service and accommodations have the potential for automation," citing self-ordering and robots as examples.[74]

Restaurants can use systems to make certain operations automatic, including food preparation, ordering, payment,

---

73 Heather Lalley, "Robot-Powered Spyce Restaurant to Close Temporarily for Revamp," Restaurant Business Online, Winsight LLC., November 15, 2019.

74 Michael Chui, James Manyika, and Mehdi Miremadi, "Where machines could replace humans—and where they can't (yet)," McKinsey Digital, McKinsey & Company, July 8, 2016.

and serving. Automation is helpful to fulfill routine tasks and collect valuable data, whether it be from online ordering or POS system analytics.[75]

Formerly CEO of a restaurant technology solution company and having extensive experience in the intersections of hospitality and technology, Brad Chun shares that "when people think about technology in restaurants, you kind of start off with the point of sale," though there is so much more to the picture.[76] He emphasizes that "surrounding that central part of the technology ecosystem, you have loyalty, mobile payments, employment management, and supply chain management. There are literally hundreds of technologies that can help you out in your business."[77] The power of automation opens doors to lift businesses in ways never imagined.

Automation in the restaurant industry supplies many benefits: reduction of error, increased speed, saving labor costs, piquing interest in customers, collecting data, and reducing food waste. It's helpful to break down the main ways automation is employed in a restaurant space, namely through front-of-house and back-of-house operations. Front-of-house examples of automation include self-order kiosks and tablets to interact with customers instead of servers or cashiers.

I once ordered and paid for overpriced lemon pepper chicken wings at a restaurant in an airport, all through a tablet. The

---

75   "National Restaurant Association Unveils its Restaurant Industry 2030 Report," National Restaurant Association, November 5, 2019.

76   Kevin Hardy, "The Digital Revolution," QSR, Journalistic, Inc., November 2014.

77   Ibid.

only communication between myself and the server was a "thank you" when they brought out the layover favorite. Human interaction for the day: check. Since so many people come and go throughout the day, it makes sense why they opted for technology versus manually writing down customer orders, especially during the busiest times.

Back-of-house examples range from automated food preparation to cleaning. In the Spyce example, front-of-house technology is demonstrated with customers ordering from a tablet, while back-of-house is seen with the actual cooking process using robots. While the typical independent restaurant may not have the resources or need to implement automation like self-order kiosks, larger chains or experience-focused small restaurants do experiment with the new technology.

While there are plenty of advantages to using automation in a restaurant, there are also some reservations to consider. One obvious hurdle is cost. Since automation is very much in its experimental stages, it will be expensive, at least initially, serving as a disadvantage to smaller restaurants in the industry. That's why it's more common to see established chains like Chili's dishing out tablets than your local mom and pop restaurant. Not only can the big players afford to test the technology, but there's also a large enough customer and employee base for it to make a substantial difference and pay off the huge price tag over time. It's an investment. That's why it is important for restaurants of all sizes to evaluate whether automation would be good for their business and whether it would be best suited in front-of-house operations, back-of-house operations, or both.

⁎ ⁎ ⁎

But how does automation affect employment? It depends on how a restaurant chooses to utilize technology, since it does matter. Naveen Joshi, founder and CEO of Allerin, a customer experience technology company, notes that "restaurants should look to strike a balance between automation and human employment while improving on their services and finances."[78] Restaurants can reap efficiency benefits from automation while also bringing out creativity and human connection. He adds that "a semi-automated restaurant with robots limited to mundane tasks can prove to be the best bet for restaurants and customers alike."[79]

Thinking about Joshi's point, automation at the moment is not necessarily to "take over" a restaurant but to drive efficiency through completing "mundane tasks." Routine tasks like flipping a burger, filling a cup of soda, or collecting payment are examples of when automation can excel. With automation, routine tasks can be accomplished faster and with less chance of error, which leaves room for human creativity and connection to be applied in other areas, such as service or menu creation. Automation does not mean humans are not needed at all but instead shifts humans to roles in the industry that can better use their skills.

In fact, a McKinsey report notes that "tighter integration with technology will free up time for human workers, including

---

78 Naveen Joshi, "Bon Appétit! Robotic Restaurants Are The Future," Forbes, Forbes Media LLC., February 3, 2020.

79 Ibid.

managers, to focus more fully on activities to which they bring skills that machines have yet to master."[80] In addition, as mentioned before, the hefty price tag means that the widespread adoption of automation will not have a jarring impact on employment right away. An estimated 1.6 million new restaurant jobs are predicted to be created by 2030, highlighting that people are still necessary in the industry.[81] So while the trend toward automation will indeed grow over time, it's not something to be immediately wary about with a balanced approach. Automation simply redefines and shifts what it means to be working at a restaurant.

* * *

Another contention with automation is the possibility of moving away from building rapport with customers, friendly service, and an atmosphere defined by the people who run the restaurant. If more and more restaurants adopt automation in their operations, then what would make one restaurant different from the next? Would the industry almost be standardized? Of course, the industry is a long way from entire operations becoming automated, considering that mostly the big chains currently fuel this trend, albeit the occasional restaurant like Spyce that leverages the novel factor of automation for smaller restaurants. But it is still important for restaurants to think of these questions to stay competitive in the long term.

---

80 "Foodservice automation drives ROI," Food Management, Informa USA, Inc., March 22, 2019.

81 "National Statistics," National Restaurant Association, accessed June 1, 2020.

For example, while Spyce largely automates its ordering and cooking process, humans serve customers the cooked bowls, which is an important step that should not be overlooked amid all the technology. To the fast-casual restaurant, the human element is what completes the experience. Spyce Chief Operating Officer Kale Rogers considers "automation as a tool to allow us to serve incredible quality to more people. A necessary component is the human touch—the presentation, the personalization, the handing it to you with a smile."[82] A human handing you a Spyce Korean bowl with a smile ends the streamlined, efficient, automated process with the magic of "human touch," finishing a customer's order in a personal way.

While Spyce prides itself on innovative technology to create delicious dishes consistently, some independent restaurants want to avoid any association with industrialized, mass-produced food and instead specialize in a particular area or master specific food and beverages, holding themselves to a certain standard. These restaurants are known as craft or artisan. While automation may play a role in their operations, it is up to humans to add value that makes it "craft" to begin with.

What makes a restaurant "craft" or "artisanal"? We've all heard of craft food and drink: at its essence, they are made from high-quality ingredients, often local, and held to a high standard of mastery. Apply this concept to the restaurants and "craft" restaurants are born.

---

82 Steve Holt, "Full service: Automation in restaurants is changing the food industry," GreenBiz, GreenBiz Group Inc., June 15, 2018.

Let's look at coffee. Some people love buying coffee from a chain like Starbucks. There are always new and interesting beverages, tasty baked delights, and for a moment, you feel special when they mispronounce your name in the endearing way they always do (the human touch). Others, however, seek independent "craft" coffee shops that use specific techniques, fine and usually local ingredients, and a distinct flair when preparing coffee. It depends on what the consumer desires, but there will always be a demand for both.

The "human touch" in the commercialized and craft forms of restaurants have different definitions, highlighting how defining what makes something "human" or of quality is relative to the consumer. Size is not necessarily an indicator of craft, which surprised me, since large chains are often associated with mass production of food while small businesses are looked upon as artisanal gems.

Patric Kuh, a distinguished restaurant critic and chef, reveals that "people should not be trapped in this fallacy of 'small is better' because artisanal is going to get bigger, and if you can maintain the standards, I think you're embodying what an artisan means, not becoming the opposite of it."[83] So it's not necessarily about size of a restaurant but rather about staying true to the craft of artisan food and drink that is its core.

Only time will tell how the rise in automation will affect the restaurant industry and how the "human element" and "restaurant craft" will carry varying definitions going forward.

---

83 Russ Parsons, "Artisan rhetoric: Patric Kuh on the growth, definition, and future of 'artisanal' food," The Splendid Table, Minnesota Public Radio, October 11, 2016.

All I will say is that as much as I enjoy a green tea Frappuccino from Starbucks, there is nothing like stepping into a corner coffee shop and enjoying the magic of a cup of chamomile tea that I know I can't find anywhere else (discussed later in this book!).

Despite all the advancements in automation in the industry, human connection still has room—even for just a stranger I'll never meet again working in a noisy, chaotic, and hectic restaurant in an airport bringing out those lemon pepper wings with a smile. Yes, the food brings joy (especially when starving after a long flight), but it's more than that. Recognizing the importance of the human element in balance with technology is how restaurants can truly take off.

MARKETING

BREAKDOWN

On road trips, I like to observe my surroundings, especially in more scenic areas. Cornfields, forests, orchards, and cattle (that we always have to point out for some reason). You also get to see the occasional billboard for a local business, fair, or event. Because these are by local companies, you'll find all sorts of things you won't find anywhere else. You can trust that the message hasn't been filtered by a team of marketing executives in a headquarters (which can be good or bad). Local companies, local outreach—there's a touch of the human spirit, if you will. Devoid of corporate influence and mass marketing. How refreshing.

A billboard for a local diner appeared while on a road trip with my family. "30 entrees $9.99 or less," it read in bold font. A plate of pancakes, eggs, and bacon joined the message. Very homestyle. The rustic and simple style added to the effect.

I tried interpreting that in different ways (I had plenty of time to spare). Did thirty entrees total cost $9.99? Wow, what a deal. You can feed your family, in-laws, neighbors, and local track team for ten bucks—in a rural part of Pennsylvania, at least. Or did it mean there are thirty entrees that cost $9.99 separately? That would equal about $300 if you bought those thirty entrees total. The more I thought about it, the more I wanted to understand the diner's intended message.

I looked up the diner on my phone and pulled up their menu: eggs, pancakes, waffles, hash browns, classic diner staples. They ended up having a bunch of items actually over $9.99. I counted their entrees (effective use of free time, I know). Fewer than thirty items were $9.99 or less. I was confused because it conflicted with the message from the billboard. Did the deal recently expire? Or was there a special menu not on the website?

And then it hit me: their phrasing motivated me to research more into their business. The fact that I was still researching that small diner twenty minutes after viewing that billboard, talking about it with my family, and reading their menu meant they accomplished their job. The next step would be to turn that initial interest in marketing into foot traffic.

I'll definitely watch out for that diner again when driving through rural Pennsylvania, and maybe I'll stop by for waffles. And get to the bottom of this $9.99 thirty-entree business.

* * *

I had the chance to talk to Oyster Sunday founder Elizabeth Tilton and Head of Projects and Client Experience Jessica Abell. "Based in New Orleans and New York City, Oyster Sunday is a corporate office for independent restaurants whose mission is to build a sustainable and supportive infrastructure for the food and beverage industry."[84] Both individuals have extensive backgrounds in hospitality. Tilton was formerly the head of brand at W&P, a culinary products company, while Abell previously worked for Danny Meyer's Union Square Hospitality Group as senior project manager of new business operations.

Both Tilton and Abell lead Oyster Sunday with the belief that "businesses of all sizes should have access to the professional services that promote healthy growth, so we're building an economy of scale that gives us all a seat at the table."[85] Tilton and Abell help businesses in the industry thrive not only in a profitable way but also in a sustainable, personal way. Their take on marketing and branding? "It's more important than ever," thanks to how technology has "catalyzed and changed the way marketing and branding impacts restaurants," Tilton said. It cannot be ignored.

Tilton shared that marketing and branding starts "the moment someone hits their smartphone," looking at restaurant social media and websites. She stressed that in "those first inter-actions, you have ten seconds to make an impact" to "tell the consumer why they should walk into your door." She contended that while the "food and beverage has to speak for itself" when customers do walk in, marketing plays an incredibly pivotal role in "the entire customer journey," from learning about the restaurant to consuming the food.

---

84 "Reimagining the hospitality industry's business infrastructure,"
    Oyster Sunday, Oyster Sunday LLC., accessed June 1, 2020.

85 "About," Oyster Sunday, Oyster Sunday LLC., accessed June 1, 2020.

Tilton and Abell also mentioned that they like to ask their clients to share their "point of view in food." They seek to advise clients, be it chefs or restaurateurs, by first learning about the core of the institution: the food. Why? Tilton and Abell shared that for Oyster Sunday clients, "food is their medium, and we're trying to figure out a way to tell the world about it." It was interesting to hear food as a "medium" since food can be more than basic sustenance for the body. It's a form of expression, a source of happiness, a vessel to connect with others. Tilton and Abell underscored that with a clear "point of view in food," it is possible to solidify a "brand identity" to help push marketing efforts. Ultimately, Tilton and Abell highlighted that "branding and marketing is an unbelievable tool to translate information" that the customer never knew and make an impact immediately, especially with the reach of technology today.

* * *

It's helpful to break down what marketing means before moving forward. According to Stanford University, marketing "is the process of planning and executing the conception, pricing, promotion, and distribution of ideas, goods, and services."[86] Part of marketing strategy, the marketing mix is a combination of factors that help deliver value to customers. The traditional marketing mix is comprised of the Four P's: Product, Price, Place, and Promotion. The four can be understood as follows:

Product: What is the product? How is it differentiated from competitors? Who is the product for? What is the service

---

86 "Marketing Strategy," Stanford University, accessed June 1, 2020.

associated with the product (warranties, etc.)? Other areas to think about in product include design, package, features, and variety.

Price: How much is a customer willing to pay? How does price affect customer perception of the product? How will discount timing and amount be applied? How does the price differ from competitors? What are payment options?

Place: How will the product be distributed? Are there multiple channels (brick-and-mortar, online, etc.) to the sell product? How accessible is it to customers?

Promotion: How is the product advertised, promoted, and communicated? Are there multiple channels (events, online, etc.) to promote the product? What is the message to convey to customers?

Some argue that the original marketing mix rings true today, though others find there is more to take into account since the mix was first introduced. The traditional Four P's can only address so much, as the entrance of technology and emphasis on individuals today mean that more factors need to be accounted for. The evolved version of the marketing mix includes two additional components: Process and People. This addition evolves the Four P's into the Six P's of the marketing mix.[87]

Process: How can data help maximize efficiency and reduce costs? How can technology be used to increase customer satisfaction and meet their needs?

---

87   Ahmad Kareh, "Evolution of The Four Ps: Revisiting The Marketing Mix," Forbes, Forbes Media LLC., January 3, 2018.

People: How do employees represent the business and its culture? What workforce is the company looking for? How can the business transaction be humanized in an era of technology?

The point of the marketing mix is to view different factors in light of each other. For example, if I sold strawberry jam, I can't just focus only on making the best strawberry jam you've ever tasted. Obviously, that's an important factor but not the only factor. I have to think about what I want it to be packaged in. Maybe plastic jars that are economical? Or glass jars that are sturdier and more attractive but pricey? And how would this difference affect customer perception and thus sales? Do I want to sell it at my local farmer's market, or perhaps over an online channel to reach a wider audience? What kind of feelings do I want to stimulate from my customers? Warmth, sense of home? How can I evoke these feelings in marketing? I'll need to collect data to see how popular my jam is among different groups of people. Who *jams* to my strawberry jam? This data will help me better define my target audience and steer promotional products to their interests. These are some ways the Six P's can be thought about, with the goal of curating a holistic marketing strategy for any business.

As Oyster Sunday's Tilton and Abell emphasized earlier, marketing, especially digitally, in the restaurant space is more influential than ever. In this section, we'll look more into the trends relating to social media, loyalty programs, and digital strategy. These areas all resonate with different parts of the marketing mix, some even with a couple at a time, something to keep in mind while reading. Even that small diner in Pennsylvania would be able to find value in these trends for exposure, interest, and reputation.

Minimize waffling and maximize waffles.

CHAPTER 8

SOCIAL MEDIA

———

"The reason I was able to grow my business was that every day, after producing thirty minutes of wine television, I spent fifteen hours a day replying to every single person's email and every single person's Twitter @ reply," Gary Vaynerchuk said on successfully growing his wine business.[88]

Who is this random person exactly and why should we care about this quote (that seems to only strain a person's eyes thanks to hours of screen time)?

Well, Gary Vaynerchuk is no stranger to people interested in marketing, communications, and entrepreneurial pursuits, catering to millions of viewers on every social media platform you can imagine. He's known for his charisma, bluntness, sharp advice, and growth mindset. Gary Vaynerchuk started getting involved with social media, business, and entrepreneurship at an early age. As he often talks about, he grew his father's wine business from 3 to 60 million dollars through marketing strategy he perfected over the years, successfully

———

88   "Gary Vaynerchuk Quotes," BrainyQuote, accessed June 1, 2020.

tapping into and retaining an audience.[89] Utilizing e-commerce and email marketing, and most importantly, connecting to his audience with meaningful content regularly, Vaynerchuk skyrocketed the success of his wine business.

Today Vaynerchuk is a lot of things and isn't afraid to share it: leader in the communications, marketing, and entrepreneurship space, current chairman of VaynerX (media and communications holding company), CEO of VaynerMedia (advertising agency), angel investor, owner of various brands, charismatic public speaker, and best-selling author.[90] Often mentioned in his talks, to grow a wine business drastically is a testament to the skill he has in his field. In other words, Vaynerchuk may know a thing or two about how to help grow one's business via marketing, though it should be taken with a grain of salt. It is worth mentioning that he has faced criticism in his drilling of "hustle" and "working hard" mentalities that supposedly offer the key to success, not considering outside factors beyond one's control and the option of living a life of balance. At the same time, he does offer a lot of motivational and useful words on marketing that help people start their own pursuits.

We can consider some of his points when we think about marketing as a whole, whether applied to an outdoor apparel company or a kebab cart. Vaynerchuk in particular is very focused on how social media can impact an individual. Forget the group. It's about *you*. Yes, you. If he can connect with you, one person,

---

89   "Gary Vaynerchuk," Gary Vaynerchuk, Gary Vee IP, LLC., accessed June 1, 2020.

90   Ibid.

that is a win. That is why he goes out of his way to form relationships. It's a relationship-first business. That's one of the "secrets" to his widely successful strategy when it comes to building an engaged and interested audience. It's the conversation, the personal impacts, to which he attributes his success.

This links to the quote from earlier. Replying to emails and Twitter replies is one of the many ways Vaynerchuk helped grow his business. Fifteen hours seems like a lot to the average person, but for him, that is what he felt was necessary so that he could form a relationship with his audience. It's not the only factor, but it is a significant factor that helped him scale his business. I personally would not measure engagement with hours inputted but rather how many people I resonated with, as it is important to balance time in a realistic way. I would focus on being effective in time rather than putting aside fifteen hours to get it done—applying Vaynerchuk's "hustle" method is not feasible for everyone. It would make sense to opt for a more realistic approach while still being ambitious in goals and following up with action.

What I do agree with is how important establishing a genuine connection with the people interacting with his content and business is. It's on an individual level—no mass replies, no general comments. It's about personalization. It's about creating some sort of kinetic energy to keep people engaged. It's about the importance of keeping the conversation going and feeling listened to. After all, marketing is that at its very core: connecting with your target audience and effectively conveying the value of your product or service. And with the help of electronic means, this can be done in a way that can reach AND resonate with hundreds, thousands, millions of people.

✳ ✳ ✳

One thing to note is that while marketing is an important part of a restaurant, it's not the only part. Great food, service, and other competitive factors are just as critical. So if a restaurant does not have great food or service, a great marketing campaign may generate interest, but it will eventually lead to more people's learning about how subpar the restaurant is. Therefore, marketing should be applied knowing a business owner can stand behind quality food, service, and atmosphere, as it ties in closely to reputation through reviews, as we will discuss later. That's when marketing is helpful for both the business (to pique interest and bring in customers) and customers (to enjoy great food and experience).

I begin with Vaynerchuk because he hosts a wildly popular Q&A video show on which people can send in their questions and seek advice from the highly dubbed marketing mastermind. He sometimes brings in experts in various industries to aid him in answering questions, so answers are fleshed out and from different viewpoints. This show is one way he can seem very approachable to his viewers and offer helpful advice for anyone tuning in, anywhere in the world. His videos are typically from a business, self-growth, entrepreneurial, or "hustler" (a term he focuses on a lot) standpoint. You'll be able to find videos on topics like how to motivate yourself in starting a business, how to use time effectively, the future of social media, or connecting with your audience—a large range of topics to help you grow yourself and your business. The interesting part about his videos is that he keeps his advice applicable to virtually any business, be it for a fashion or a construction company. The basic principles of marketing are the same, though the fine-tuned details would be different based on the industry. In 2019, Vaynerchuk uploaded an episode on YouTube that dove into restaurant marketing. Stay tuned to learn about interesting nuggets of information to take away.

In his informative episode "How to Market a Restaurant on Social Media," from GaryVee TV on YouTube, Vaynerchuk and Jon Taffer answer a call-in question specifically about restaurants.[91] Jon Taffer is a highly regarded consultant and entrepreneur in the entertainment, hospitality, and nightlife industries, helping companies with marketing strategy, customer acquisition, and more.[92] You may have heard of him as the host and producer for the show *Bar Rescue* on Paramount Network in which he works to save unsuccessful bars with the help of his expertise in business.[93] You could say he really sets the *bar*. Didn't enjoy that pun? I'm not em*bar*rassed about it. Jokes aside, Vaynerchuk and Taffer teamed up to help answer questions in this restaurant-focused episode.

On that episode, caller Chandler Lyles, owner of Lyles BBQ Company, sought advice on how he can grow his business and gain interest from the public using social media.[94] While his business has been profitable, beginning as a tent and then shifting to a brick-and-mortar location, Lyles aims to work on improving his social media presence to grow his business

91 *GaryVee TV*, "How to Market a Restaurant on Social Media," January 16, 2019, video, 18:25.

92 "About Jon Taffer," Jon Taffer, Jon Taffer, LLC, accessed June 1, 2020.

93 Ibid.

94 *GaryVee TV*, "How to Market a Restaurant on Social Media," January 16, 2019, video, 18:25.

even more. After all, marketing is in the media. And money is in the marketing. So where do you go? Media.

Taffer started by stating that Lyles should work on creating reactions—garnering curiosity from people.[95] How can you use social media to make people curious about your product? At the physical restaurant, how do people respond to the food? What is the story behind your product, your business? The first thing to consider is the reaction from the audience by means of curiosity and story both in person and online, making it interesting so that it isn't just any barbeque place.

Vaynerchuk added that the "environment around food culture" is "dominated by consumption online," stressing the importance for restaurants to not only be on social media but be *regular* on social media.[96] At one point, Vaynerchuk suddenly pulls up the Instagram account for Lyles BBQ Company, aghast that the last time he posted was *four* days prior to the call. For an average person using Instagram, four days ago may seem very recent. But in context of business, that's four days lost in getting a "reaction" from people. Four days lost in selling his story and the quality of that product and in keeping the kinetic energy going. On top of that, Taffer homed in on investing in quality photos of different parts of the business, like the process of smoking or meat preparation. It's all about letting the viewers in on what goes down in barbeque town. So it's not only about posting a lot but also about the quality of what you post. Always ask yourself if what you're posting is adding value.

---

95   Ibid.

96   Ibid.

After reviewing his social media activity, Vaynerchuk urged Lyles to step it up by posting more frequently on more platforms.[97] At the end of the episode, Vaynerchuk's advice to the Lyle's barbeque business was to put out a video on a daily basis, upload four posts on Instagram, seven on Twitter, and five on Facebook, and start a barbeque podcast to which content is uploaded once a week. He also mentioned using hashtags so that more people can be exposed to the content and messaging people who tag the same area of the business personally with a "get x free" deal. This deal would increase the likelihood of them checking out the business (because it is in their area and they get something for free), possibly posting it and sharing it with their audience, and spreading word-of-mouth marketing. As discussed in a different part of this book, it is very difficult (and expensive) to attract customers, so the goal is to wring in potential customers with something for free or with discounts, increase chances of upselling, and get them to come back for a second time.

Some may think that this strategy is aggressive. Too much social media? Will it be for naught? But considering how Vaynerchuk invested so much time in social media in building his wine business, there is a reason why he pushes individuals with businesses to leverage social media like he did. Of course, parts of his advice are tailored to Lyles' own case and cannot be applied universally. But we, as a general audience, can take away the importance of regularly posting quality content on multiple platforms, framing a story to connect with people, and cultivating interest with targeted marketing.

---

97   Ibid.

Let's shift gears to different aspects of marketing relevant today.

The idea of someone documenting their experience (videos, posts, tweets, reviews, photos) on social media (Instagram, Facebook, Twitter, Yelp) is UGC, or user-generated content.[98] The content comes from the customer, not from the business itself. A photo taken by a restaurant employee would not be UGC, but a customer's photo of the food they ate there would be. UGC is also an example of a type of social proof that leads a person to trust another person simply because they have experienced that product or service.

I had a few friends in college who loved all things acai. My friend Anoushka, in particular, would never fail to post on social media about her latest trip to Playa Bowls, an eatery near Boston College that specializes in acai, pitaya, coconut bowls, and more. Anoushka would even make her own bowl combinations from scratch, evidencing her passion for the nutritious and flavorful treat. Those vibrant photos and positive descriptions raving about how fresh and delicious it was motivated me to try it for the very first time. And boy, did those brilliant bowls live up to her reviews.

If the business itself were to post about its bowl offerings, it would be easy to dismiss the post as a promotion. But because someone I knew personally vouched for the food, I was more inclined to try it. Another customer confirming a product's or service's quality is more valuable in a customer's

---

98 "Restaurant Social Media Marketing Trends," Gourmet Marketing, accessed June 1, 2020.

decision-making process.[99] In fact, a spontaneous trip to Playa Bowls with my friends Ivana and Prashanti was how I said goodbye to my sophomore year on campus. Had my acai-loving friends never shared their enthusiasm about it over social media, I would never had been able to share such a special moment with close friends. There's nothing like goji berry-topped chia bowls drizzled with honey and good company.

* * *

While UGC is largely in the hands of the customer, paid advertising has been a go-to way for businesses to take control of their marketing efforts, on Facebook, in particular. As of 2019, about 2.6 billion people accessed Facebook monthly and 7 million advertisers actively used its services.[100] Advertisers cannot reach out to all 2.6 billion people, nor should they have to. Facebook provides the tools so advertisers can cater to a specific audience with a message as effectively as possible. This is an investment. It takes money to use Facebook ad tools, including access to custom or relevant audiences, optimization options like cost per click (paying each time a person clicks on an ad), and advertising during busy times of the year.[101]

Restaurants that can adjust are essential in communicating with a specific audience. On top of the help of Facebook ads, a business's page itself is also important. There, one can

---

99   Ibid.

100   "Insights to Go," Facebook for Business, accessed June 1, 2020.

101   Gary Henderson, "How Much Do Facebook Ads Cost?" *Digital Marketing Blog, DigitalMarketing.org,* September 21, 2018.

easily upload menus, interact with followers, post photos, host contests, and promote deals.[102] One trend weaved in with social media is an emphasis on branding, establishing a personal connection. This connects to the story idea from Vaynerchuk's video with Taffer. Customers are interested in the roots of a business, the story behind a dish, and what makes it special, so the idea is to curate a "brand voice" that honors interactivity and authenticity. Don't just post, but post with purpose. Engage. Social media food influencers do just that.

When it comes to social media, we can't *not* talk about influencer marketing.[103] Individuals with a large social media following can expose their wide audience to a new product or service. If an "influencer" is large enough and shares the product or service effectively, they can be compensated with cash, discounts, or free products. Because many influencers are paid for access to their audience base, there is a conversation about how to truly measure engagement and if it is worth paying influencers in the first place. Whether investing in influencers is an effective marketing tool is debatable and subject to the business itself.

To learn more about food influencing, I spoke with Maya Taha, a college student who runs the growing food Instagram account @mayathefoodie. She has accumulated over 7,000 followers, posting delicious photos of everything from brisket burgers in Lebanon to coconut cakes in Boston. An avid cook and baker,

---

102 "How Restaurants Can Effectively Use Social Media Marketing,"
    WebFX, accessed June 1, 2020.

103 Brent Barnhart, "The most important social media trends to know for
    2020," SproutSocial, Sprout Social, Inc., May 6, 2020.

she even posts recipes and photos of her own creations. My favorite part of Taha's account is that she showcases a diverse set of restaurants and foods in whatever city she finds herself in. Perfectly crispy dosa, homemade Nutella-stuffed doughnuts, Afghan mantu, tuna tataki, you name it—Taha is not afraid to try new things and share it with the world.

Taha began her food-centered social media account to marry her passions of discovering delicious food and photography. She kicked off her journey by visiting places she "thought were cool posting" and featuring on her account.

After she gained a significant amount of followers, Taha shared that "restaurants started reaching out to me" and "messaging me, asking if I would want to come try out new menu items, or if I wanted to collaborate with a giveaway of my thoughts." Gaining exposure to Taha's food-loving followers, restaurants in the area find her to be the perfect person to reach out to.

Taha shared more about the process. When a restaurant invites her, she's greeted by the owner, manager, or someone "higher up in the restaurant." Taha takes time discussing the founding and general information about the eatery. Then, the food: "They ask me to pick whatever I want" from the menu, Taha shared. Or, they "will just fill the table with food" for Taha to have her pick at. Sometimes, restaurants will host "influencer events" for the community to get together, something Taha finds to be fun and mutually beneficial for influencers and restaurants.

But Taha revealed her account is about more than just posting a mouthwatering photo. It takes time and effort. She "likes and comments on other people's pictures" to engage with the food community, makes sure to "do research" when a restaurant reaches out to collaborate before agreeing to it, and spends about twenty to thirty minutes on photography to ensure that she captures the best shot in proper lighting. "It's a lot of work," Taha concluded.

Taha placed emphasis on connecting with people. She enjoys interacting with her followers, whether it be through talking about the "origins of food" or about what different foods are called in other cultures. She finds "the bonding aspect" of her account to be a critical one with a global reach.

While Taha's account is smaller compared to the other food accounts boasting hundreds of thousands of followers, she still can create impact for restaurants. I asked her if any of her followers ended up checking out any of the restaurants she posted to understand just how effective it was. "All the time," she responded enthusiastically.

"Once I posted this tea I was drinking," Taha started. "And a bunch of people went out and tried it" and sent her photos of the same tea. You could say her posts resonate with her followers very matcha (I'm guil-tea of "bad" puns). Anyway, Taha told me that her followers will try recipes or restaurants she posts on the account and "almost always tell me about it." Fostering that level of engagement is critical in keeping the account relevant, interesting, and personal.

So while Taha's account may not be the biggest player in the game, she still adds tremendous value through connecting and sharing the joy of food with others, in turn generating business for restaurants, all while having fun, channeling her love of photography, and enjoying good food.

For businesses, communicating their story over social media is critical, especially with so much competition. Say it's a pizza shop in Brooklyn that has been passed on for generations. You might find those every other block, so it's time to take social media seriously. Is the restaurant marketer or owner posting on Instagram about its famous Mediterranean pizza with quality, mouthwatering shots? Opportunity for influencers to post about it? A video about their famous wood-fired pizza oven that shows the cooking process? A Facebook ad that perhaps targets middle-aged, food-loving people interested in food who live in New York? A tweet about the pizza special happening that day? Not forgetting hashtags? Offering promotions to people in the area with personal messaging? Responding to replies on any social media posts? Linking social media accounts on a main website? The avenues are endless. When I look up the hashtag #newyorkpizza on Instagram, over 117,000 posts pop up. By the time you're reading this, probably even more are out there!

With the power of social media, imagine how much more interest doing all these steps would garner. A business wants and needs that interest to survive. Bring in new customers and make sure they stay. Remember that even if a business does all this but still experiences little foot traffic, the issue may be elsewhere, maybe in the food, service, location, or experience. Then again, if a business does all this and ends up popular on social media, this does not necessarily mean that it's the best business in the game. It means that it has a higher chance to prove to the customer that it is good at its job because it piques interest. At the end of the day, success is just as much about getting a customer through the door (with the help of marketing) as it is about keeping them returning (through a good experience). Use marketing wisely.

CHAPTER 9

LOYALTY PROGRAMS

———

As an avid lover of Chipotle, I am currently enrolled in Chipotle Rewards, the fast-casual chain's free loyalty program.[104] (Disclaimer: this is not an ad, and I am not sponsored! At least as of 2020. I just really love their burrito bowls.) Each purchase at Chipotle earns me points. With the current point distribution, I can earn ten points for every $1 spent. Once I earn 1,250 points, I earn a free entree at Chipotle. Because I frequent Chipotle enough, I figured I might as well gain something out of each purchase anyway to "earn" a meal later. But for restaurants that I go to once in a blue moon, subscribing to their loyalty program just would not make sense. On the other hand, would it encourage me to go more often? Let's dive into how effective loyalty programs are as a marketing strategy.

Loyalty programs are helpful in a time with immense restaurant competition. Sallie Burnett, founder of Customer Insight Group, who has over twenty-five years of customer loyalty experience, emphasizes that "customers are quick to jump to

———

104 "Chipotle Rewards," Chipotle Mexican Grill, accessed June 1, 2020.

a competitor if they are offered coupons or other discounts, but restaurant customer loyalty programs can ensure that they keep coming back."[105] Additionally, with a loyalty program in place, "65 percent of members feel like the brand rewards their loyalty," making them feel valued.[106] When the customer feels valued, they are more willing to give the customer experience a higher rating, recommend the brand to others, spend more, pay a higher price, and take advantage of "non-transactional" rewards like discounts or "experiential rewards" like a cooking class.[107] Solidifying that connection with the customer with an impactful loyalty program is incredibly powerful.

* * *

Loyalty programs carry many benefits for businesses. They help increase the number of visits of customers, create a connection with customers, collect information about purchasing habits, preferences, and demographics, identify trends in behavior and responses, retarget, upsell, and cross-sell.[108] I'll go into what the last three terms mean and why they are helpful.

Retargeting is advertising based on a target customer's previous actions to drive interest. Adam Guild, the CEO of

---

105 Sallie Burnett, "Restaurants Serve Up Loyalty Programs to Combat Competition," Forbes, Forbes Media LLC., March 25, 2019.

106 Emily Collins, "How Consumers Really Feel About Loyalty Programs," Forrester, Forrester Research, Inc., May 8, 2017.

107 Ibid.

108 Slava, Ponomarov, "Great Restaurant Loyalty Apps and How to Build One," QSR Magazine, Journalistic, Inc., September 2019.

Placepull, a restaurant marketing company, noted that past customers and website visitors are the two types of people to focus on. Because past customers have already visited the restaurant before (the hard part), "all they need is a reminder of your restaurant to get them to come back the next time they dine out."[109] This reminder can take the form of advertising, be it through Facebook or Google. As for website visitors who haven't purchased, Guild urged that "it's important to use an ad that gets their attention, is relevant to them, and calls them to action."[110] Some ways to retarget include speaking to a specific set of people, sharing something relevant with a sense of urgency, and sharing an easy "call to action" with a link.

One example of retargeting is if you visited the Panera Bread website and browsed without ordering anything. Because you expressed interest by simply visiting, Panera would try to win you with retargeting efforts. You'll soon find Panera ads on different websites, even ones completely unrelated to Panera Bread. The goal of this is to draw customers back to the online platform and make a purchase.

Upselling is encouraging a customer to buy upgrades on top of what is being purchased.[111] An example of upselling in a loyalty program is if adding whipped cream to hot chocolate would be an additional cost. A customer may be more inclined to make this purchase on top of the hot chocolate because they would only be adding more points to be put to

---

109 Adam Guild, "How to Use Your Retargeting to Grow Your Restaurant Revenue," Forbes, Forbes Media LLC., July 16, 2019.

110 Ibid.

111 "Upselling," Shopify, accessed June 1, 2020.

use later. Another is a cashier pushing a larger drink since it is only fifty cents more.

Cross-selling is encouraging a customer to make additional product or service purchases.[112] A classic case is if you order a burger and the server asks, "Do you want fries with that?" to push the sale of an additional item. This simple question can drive the purchase of additional items, something that chains like McDonald's (fries) and Chipotle (guacamole) take advantage of and that helps in their success. Loyalty programs can help cross-sell by motivating customers to buy more on their own to gain points, motivated by exclusive product offerings, or to complement an existing purchase. Yes, I do want fries with my burger.

* * *

It's not all sunshine and daisies, however. Loyalty programs can be detrimental if not checked and measured periodically. It is critical for businesses to keep loyalty programs easy, convenient, interesting, accessible, and financially beneficial.

Potential cons of loyalty programs include maintenance according to customer needs, cost if rewards are too large, and difficulty managing data.[113] If a business takes necessary steps to protect against these pitfalls (see later with measuring loyalty program success), such programs create significant value for both customers and businesses alike.

112　Ibid.

113　Jim Granat, "The Pros and Cons of Instituting a Customer Loyalty Program," Forbes, Forbes Media LLC., September 3, 2020.

Loyalty programs also take different forms. In the past, more traditional methods were popular: punch cards and redeeming offers through receipts.[114] Now with technology, newer forms of programs are gaining more traction, through POS systems, mobile apps, credit cards, and even by phone number.

Customers can subscribe to loyalty programs through a business' POS system, like Square.[115] If you've ever had a business ask for your email or phone number for points, that was a loyalty program embedded in its point-of-sale system. Customers receive points automatically with every purchase. These points and additional offers are sent to customers through email. The perk about this type of program is that customers do not have to expend additional energy and the store tracks the points. Yay.

In contrast to POS system loyalty programs, customers have more control when they download a company's loyalty program app and create an account. While the POS subscription system does offer personalization of offers based on purchasing habits, a mobile app takes a loyalty program a step further by allowing customers to check points and even conduct purchases easily.[116]

An example of one of the most popular rewards programs in the restaurant industry is Starbucks Rewards, boasting

---

114 "Restaurant Loyalty Programs," WebstaurantStore, WebsaurantStore Food Service Equipment and Supply Company, April 26, 2019.

115 Ibid.

116 Ibid.

over 16 million members as of early 2019.[117] Once signed up for Starbucks Rewards through the app or online, a member earns two Stars for every dollar spent.[118] With more purchases, Stars accumulate so the member can eventually redeem food and drinks. The company also offers a Starbucks Visa Card to spend and collect Stars, helpful in adding another medium of using the loyalty program based on what customers prefer.

Their current Star redemption distribution is as follows:[119]

- 25 Stars = Customized drink (add or substitute an ingredient)

- 50 Stars = Brewed hot coffee, bakery item, or hot tea

- 150 Stars = Handcrafted drink, hot breakfast, or parfait

- 200 Stars = Lunch salad, protein box, or salad

- 400 Stars = Select merchandise or at-home coffee

What makes Starbucks Rewards so popular is that the company keeps it easy, interesting, and personalized. Starbucks Rewards embodies key aspects of a strong loyalty program that contribute to its success.[120]

---

117 "Starbucks to enhance industry-leading Starbucks Rewards loyalty program," Starbucks Stories and News, Starbucks Corporation., March 19, 2019.

118 Ibid.

119 "Starbucks Rewards," Starbucks Coffee Company, accessed June 1, 2020.

120 Sallie Burnett, "Restaurants Serve Up Loyalty Programs to Combat Competition," Forbes, Forbes Media LLC., March 25, 2019.

- *It's easy and convenient.* The program is "frictionless" because it uses technology. Unlike traditional methods that require high-effort from the customer with cards, Starbucks Rewards gives members a preference of using the loyalty program via app or online. Whipping out a phone to redeem stars is much easier than fishing in your wallet for ten minutes trying to find a punch card. It's especially easy because a member can use the app to order and pay ahead, accumulating Stars instantly. Alternatively, a member can upload their receipt online after purchase to collect Stars. This ensures that the program is accessible regardless of time of purchase or mode of technology. On top of that, members can start redeeming within two to three visits, bringing value to the member immediately.

- *It's interesting and engaging.* The loyalty program is interesting because the company doesn't just stop at converting Stars to rewards but also brings more to the table. A member in the loyalty program can enjoy free brewed coffee and tea refills, Double-Star days, Bonus Stars, games, and early or extended offers that nonmembers would not have access to.[121] These features keep members engaged and excited in the process of collecting points, ultimately wanting to come back for more.

- *It's tailored and personalized.* Personalization is also an important part of the loyalty program. First, members are gifted a Birthday Reward celebrating their special day every year.[122] This makes the customer feel special and

---

121 "Starbucks Rewards," Starbucks Coffee Company, accessed June 1, 2020.

122 "Starbucks' Rewards Terms of Use," Starbucks Coffee Company, August 19, 2019.

"seen" by a company as large as Starbucks. Second, the program pushes personalized offerings and coupons so members can have a more tailored experience based on their search and buying behavior.[123] These special offers are based on members' respective preferences and data so Starbucks can better attract and retain customers.

MEASURING SUCCESS

Say you have a loyalty program in place. How can you gauge the success of a loyalty program? Upserve's Kristin Crane explains five key measurements: consumer retention rate, negative churn, net promoter score, customer effort score, and up-trending.[124] Get ready, because now it gets a little bit technical!

First, consumer retention rate. Are customers returning to the restaurant after enrolling in the program? Is there a difference in sales for members and nonmembers over time? A change in consumer retention rate has a significant impact on profit.

A Bain & Company analysis with Earl Sasser of Harvard Business School found that an increase of 5 percent in the consumer retention rate grows the profits by 25 percent to 95 percent.[125] That was in 1990. Thanks to the technology of today, new customer acquisition and retention strategies

---

123 Ibid.

124 Kristin Crane, "How Restaurants Are Using Loyalty Programs to Boost Business," Upserve, Upserve, Inc., July 20, 2018.

125 Frederick F. Reichheld and Phil Schefter, "The Economics of E-Loyalty," Harvard Business School, President & Fellows of Harvard College, June 7, 2000.

emerge to drive profit. Now it's easier than ever to let some-one know your thoughts about the phone case you bought from Amazon with reviews or send someone the link of a cool restaurant you found downtown. It's easy to spread information about a product or service, refer new customers, establish a loyal following, and more. Therefore, a loyalty program conducted over technology, like a mobile app, has great potential for increasing the consumer retention rate.

For people who like math, an equation can help visualize this. The consumer retention rate (CRR) can be calculated as shown below:[126]

Let:

Number of customers at the end of the period = E

Number of new customers acquired during the period = A

Number of customers at the start of the period = S

Formula:

(E-A)/(S) * 100

It's easier to think of an example. Say you just opened a bakery that established a reputation for its scrumptious strawberry shortcakes over the first couple of months. Let's say that you began the period with about 40 customers (S), gained 30 more

---

126 Kristin Crane, "How Restaurants Are Using Loyalty Programs to Boost Business," Upserve, Upserve, Inc., July 20, 2018.

during the period (A), and lost 10 customers by the end of
the period. The total number of customers at the end of the
period (E) would be 60 by adding beginning customers with
new customers and subtracting lost customers. 40+30-10 =
60. After finding E, we plug it in the formula as follows:

$$(60-30)/(40)*100 = 75 \text{ percent}$$

Having calculated the CRR, what does it mean? The ideal
CRR would be 100 percent, but to retain every single existing
customer is not what happens in reality. Instead, the CRR
understood in context of benchmarks.[127] One benchmark
could be comparing how the rate changes over time within
the company itself. Another is by comparing a competitor's
rate or trends against one's own company. It depends on the
goals of a business for what makes a "good" CRR, though it
should ideally be as high as possible.[128] So your bakery's retention rate can be good or poor depending on the benchmark.

Loyalty programs help raise the CRR as it attracts and keeps
customers. Only if such programs are able to add another layer
of value to a customer's shopping experience are customers
more inclined to purchase or return.

The second way to gauge success is through negative churn.
What is the rate of customers leaving the restaurant? The
churn rate measures how often a customer leaves or terminates

---

127 Dan Virgillito, "How to Calculate Customer Retention Rate (and
     Improve Yours)," *Cooper Chronicles (Blog), Cooper CRM, Inc.,*
     September 27, 2018.

128 Kostas Papageorgiou, "5 Must Have Customer Retention Metrics,"
     Userlike, August 31, 2016.

business with a company. A company's goal is to foster negative churn so that customers stay interested and loyal.[129] According to Upserve, companies can find out whether customers are invested in the loyalty program by "tracking when loyalty members are returning more often, spending more in a single visit, participating in more events or higher-priced services and products" and comparing this information to that of nonmembers.[130] A loyalty program has potential for negative churn, critical for restaurants to keep customers coming through the door.

Third, net promoter score. The net promoter score (NPS), first introduced by Bain & Company, is an index from -100 to 100 that measures how willing a customer is to recommend a service or product to others.[131] NPS is used to scope how satisfied customers are with a product or service along with how loyal they are to it. Companies use surveys as the medium to help collect this information.

You're probably familiar with being asked how likely you are to recommend the product or service to others from a scale of 0 to 10, be it through a survey you find on your receipt or after you make an online purchase. If a customer rates it lower than or equal to 6, they are called "detractors." The title indicates that they would likely not purchase from the company again. Medallia notes that detractors can "potentially damage the company's reputation through

---

129 Jake Frankenfield, "Churn Rate," Investopedia, Dotdash, May 25, 2020.

130 Kristin Crane, "How Restaurants Are Using Loyalty Programs to Boost Business," Upserve, Upserve, Inc., July 20, 2018.

131 "Net Promoter Score," Medallia, accessed June 1, 2020.

negative word of mouth."[132] If a customer rates it a 7 or 8, this means that while the customer may be satisfied, there is a chance for the customer to switch to a competitor's offering. This group is called "passives," meaning they would neither spread positive nor negative opinions of the product or service—not solidly loyal. Customers who rate a 9 or 10 are the most satisfied of customers, the customers who would return to the company and promote the product or service to others. We call them "promoters."

I, for one, am a *promoter* of a doughnut chain called Duck Donuts—their fresh, warm, and rich doughnuts never disappoint (you should check them out). Anyway, the three different categories of customers—detractors, passives, and promoters—help us better understand customer loyalty by calculating the Net Promoter Score.

The NPS is found by subtracting detractors (percentage of those who do not recommend the product or service) from promoters (those who do recommend it). The higher the customer rating, the higher the net promoter score, the goal a loyalty program hopes to achieve.

The fourth factor to assess loyalty program success is the customer effort score (CES).[133] How much effort does a customer have to put in to receive a good experience? A company's goal is to make a customer input as little effort as possible. Executive Advisor at Gartner, Sarah Dibble, affirmed that "if you

---

132 Ibid.

133 Kristin Crane, "How Restaurants Are Using Loyalty Programs to Boost Business," Upserve, Upserve, Inc., July 20, 2018.

can only measure one thing, it should be effort," because, "our research finds that effort is the strongest driver to customer loyalty."[134] So we know there is a connection. But could it really be impactful?

Yes, yes, it can. *The Effortless Experience: Conquering the New Battleground for Customer Loyalty*, Matthew Dixon, Nick Toman, and Rick DeLisi's book that dives into customer loyalty, mentions that "96 percent of customers with a high-effort service interaction become more disloyal compared to just 9 percent who have a low-effort experience. Disloyal customers are likely to cost the company more — they spread negative word of mouth and cease future purchases."[135] A customer can find something high-effort if it requires any additional action or responsibility on their part or if a transaction was difficult for whatever reason.

Coupons, punch cards, and other additional items that ultimately require effort on the customer's part constitute as high-effort.[136] This reminds me of the time when a restaurant handed me a punch card with the offer to "buy 9 smoothies, get the 10th free!" It would have worked out great if I didn't lose the card the next day. Well, that offer went out the window really fast. In order to realize the value of the offer, the first step would be to keep it with me every time I go to that specific restaurant: high-effort. Paper coupons also have the

---

134 Jordan Bryan, "What's Your Customer Effort Score?" Gartner, Gartner, Inc., February 11, 2020.

135 "What is Customer Effort Score (CES) & How Do I Measure It?" Qualtrics, accessed June 1, 2020.

136 Kristin Crane, "How Restaurants Are Using Loyalty Programs to Boost Business," Upserve, Upserve, Inc., July 20, 2018.

same effect. Searching in newspapers, magazines, and more to find a great coupon for a product you've had your eyes on, only to lose the slip of paper somewhere in your house and find it approximately seven months later while trying to find something else is high-effort. Finding alternate means of bringing in customers without the need for the customer to expend effort is key to maximizing the loyalty necessary to drive profit.

To calculate the CES, the first step is to send out a CES survey after interaction with the customer.[137] It most commonly takes the form of the Likert Scale (Agree, Strongly Agree, etc.), a 1 to 10 scale, a 1 to 5 scale, or emotion faces (☺). The survey poses a question or statement relating to how easy the customer found a transaction to be. Because there are different survey types, what constitutes as a "good" CES score differs for each scale. But all associations toward "more ease" and "less effort" in these respective survey types would be strong. This data is helpful in getting a sense of how customers feel after interacting with the company.

A loyalty program in which customer effort is low is key in its effectiveness. Using mobile apps for loyalty programs has increased in popularity, thanks to their ease compared to traditional punch cards and coupons. Just download the app, input information, and follow the instructions on how to make the most of a certain rewards program. But does this mean there is no chance for it to be high-effort by being mobile? No. Even the most rewarding of loyalty programs

---

137 Tim, "What is Customer Effort Score (CES) & How to Measure It?" Customer Success (Blog), Retently, December 6, 2018.

can also risk being high-effort if a customer has to input a lot of information, is confused with unclear instructions, must navigate a difficult interface, or must face other additional complications or responsibilities. It is up to restaurants to devise a loyalty program that is both easy for the customer to participate in and beneficial for the restaurant as a whole.

Fifth, up-trending. Up-trending is when data moves upward, and in this case, if there is an increase in the number of loyalty program members across time. Upserve gives this example: "If you are looking at total visits to your restaurant for a year-long period, comparing 'months 1 through 6' to 'months 7 through 12' should display an increase in loyalty program members in the latter months."[138] There should be an upward trend of visits for members to prove that the loyalty program is in fact working. It is also important to "take note of trends and adjust your marketing if you don't see positive results," viewing visits in context.[139] A trend from Toast that helps with up-trending is that "on average, visitation frequency increases by 75 percent between a customer's first reward and their tenth reward."[140] Having the program in the first place already pushes a customer to visit more, which is great for business.

Consumer retention rate, negative churn, net promoter score, customer effort score, and up-trending are five ways of measuring how successful a loyalty program is. Using

---

138 Kristin Crane, "How Restaurants Are Using Loyalty Programs to Boost Business," Upserve, Upserve, Inc., July 20, 2018.

139 Ibid.

140 Julia Beebe, "Whip Your Restaurant Loyalty Program Into Shape [Infographic]," Toast, Toast, Inc., February 13, 2018.

these analytics, restaurants can better tailor their efforts to successfully attract and retain customers for the long run.

Loyalty programs taking advantage of current technology is the future and brings numerous benefits to a business. Keeping customers interested is even more important than bringing new ones through the door. In fact, it is five times more expensive to reel in new customers than it is to retain existing customers.[141] Therefore, businesses should look toward maximizing their existing customer base and focus efforts on converting people who rarely make purchases to keep loyal customers for the long term.

---

141 Jia Wertz, "Don't Spend 5 Times More Attracting New Customers, Nurture The Existing Ones," Forbes, Forbes Media LLC., September 12, 2018.

CHAPTER 10

DIGITAL STRATEGY

My stomach growls, sending a message known since the beginning of time. It's time to eat. I'm out of the house, so what restaurant should I go to? I crack my knuckles, determined to appease my hunger with tried-and-true search methods: the internet and technology, of course. I whip out my phone and consult Google reviews and Yelp. I scroll. Hmm, that restaurant seems to have reviews on either extreme. A little iffy—keep scrolling. Oh! This one has a five-star rating! Wait, only two people gave a review. Not representative at all. Keep scrolling. Hmm, this one has a four-and-a-half-star rating with over one hundred reviews. Let me read a couple. Wow, almost everyone raves about those spicy noodles. The pictures look really good, too. It's within budget, and nearby. I'll give this place a shot.

The first thing I do when it's time to decide what restaurant to eat at is consult reviews online. I like to conduct my research and weigh the options. What did customers think about the service? Food? Cleanliness? Quality? Price? What can I learn from pictures with the review? I browse online reviews religiously until I am able to find the perfect location to satisfy my appetite. It's a process. I'm not the only person who does this. In fact, 90 percent of customers read online reviews before deciding where to eat.[142] So it's important for restaurants to establish a reputation online to attract new customers. This reputation can range from Google reviews to Yelp to Foursquare to other platforms. But other factors beyond just having a great review bring in customers.

Dan Strutt, co-Founder at App.Foundation and Sappsuma, put a particular focus on Google reviews. How a restaurant is ranked has influence on how a customer sees the restaurant in the first place, linked to search engine optimization (SEO).[143] SEO is the process of increasing traffic and exposure of visitors to one's website by ranking high in searches organically (without paying).[144] Strutt affirmed that "when searching for local businesses online, users are now shown Google review ratings for local businesses BEFORE websites. A steady stream of online reviews is viewed by Google as a source of trustworthiness and authority."[145] Having the reviews and restaurants pop up as a top hit in searches is helpful for businesses. Therefore, it is especially important for restaurants to make sure they allocate attention in bettering their ranking, as "the better your SEO," Strutt explained, "the higher your website is ranked when users search for local businesses."[146]

---

142 Holly Everett, "Digital Marketing for Restaurants: How to Get Found Online," Upserve, Upserve, Inc., January 31, 2019.

143 Andreea Dobrila, "Growing Restaurant Trends in 2019, According to Industry Experts," GloriaFood, Global Food Tech SRL., January 28, 2019.

144 Britney Muller, "SEO 101," Moz, Moz Inc., accessed June 1, 2020.

145 Andreea Dobrila, "Growing Restaurant Trends in 2019, According to Industry Experts," GloriaFood, Global Food Tech SRL., January 28, 2019.

146 Ibid.

I had the chance to speak with Maciej Godlewski, senior manager of digital marketing at Higher Logic. Godlewski has immense experience in all things online marketing, including web analytics and SEO strategy.

What's interesting is that our conversation all started with a college interview in high school. Assigned as my interviewer, Godlewski and I met at a craft gelato shop in Washington, DC, where I first learned about his love for biographies, passion for renewable energy, and work in the digital marketing space. I also learned how incredibly refreshing pineapple gelato tastes. Fast forward to a couple years later when I started writing this book, pondering who it would be interesting to talk to and learn from. Godlewski immediately came to mind. Full circle.

Godlewski shared that one critical part of digital marketing strategy, from SEO to social media, is that it is not an "instant solution." It is largely experimental, and "to do it well, you have to constantly keep tracking and keep changing goals" while also "measuring if you're performing to the goals," he explained. In other words, a lot of moving parts lend themselves to a constant revision process.

I asked about how a business should go about strengthening their strategy and SEO. Can individual businesses do it themselves or should they consult experienced professionals? Godlewski said it really depends. Sometimes if businesses have the time and money, or "internal bandwith," they can train or hire skilled employees. Because "the beginnings are slow," newer businesses would often try to do it themselves, Godlewski added. However, he brought up that "other times, businesses do require either agencies or contractors to come in and do it," if they are "really serious about it." Differences in how important SEO is to a business and what resources they can invest leads to various approaches in how to better digital marketing efforts. If restaurants want to thrive from showcasing positive reviews and securing a high search ranking, it is clear why they would find a stronger SEO and digital marketing strategy imperative to attracting customers.

As for social media, Godlewski advised that adding a focused approach is the way to go when starting. He broke it down in three points, a helpful framework.

First, businesses must be clear on a target audience, since "social media has always been focused on where your audience is." Without having a vision of who a potential customer or consumer would be, implementing effective digital strategy is difficult and costly.

Second, businesses should identify a handful of platforms that cater to that specific audience. Certain platforms are more effective for different types of people. After all, "there's no point if your audience isn't on social media networks that much," Godlewski mentioned, emphasizing the importance of linking the audience and the platform tightly. Be where your target market is. In addition, he suggested focusing on two primary platforms to avoid "trying to do everything" and overextending yourself with more cost than benefit.

Third, businesses must assess the time and capital they have to "maintain it and actually give it a good effort, versus a very scattered approached." While Godlewski's points do not speak to just the restaurant industry specifically, digital marketing tools are helpful for all sorts of businesses, regardless of industry. To summarize his main points on getting started: know your audience, know where your audience is active, and know the amount you can invest.

Besides SEO and social media, there are an abundance of tools for businesses to use. One that has great power and growth is email outreach. Godlewski shared with me that a lot of companies are "using marketing automation platforms to figure out how to send emails and also maintain large databases of people they can reach out to." There are so many new, automated ways to reach out to a target audience, with email marketing being one that should not be overlooked. He revealed that it is "so powerful because once you have someone's permission to email them," you can reach out at "very low costs." This struck me because it highlights just how accessible it is for virtually any business, big or small, in any industry.

It also reminded me how I'm subscribed to so many businesses newsletters, through which they can push their product or service. An apparel company's flashy new deal, a restaurant's limited-time offer—what's in your email inbox? Mine includes a lot of Chipotle emails. It was actually an email that led me to discover and download the Chipotle app, join the loyalty program, and make additional purchases through that. Taco 'bout effective marketing.

Digital strategy, while taking great time and experimentation, can help restaurants reap benefits: clearer direction, a ground for differentiation, better understanding of the market and customer, and more, especially since reviews, rankings, and social media presence are so important for exposure and engagement.[147] The next time you visit a restaurant, think about how its online presence and activity may have played a role in your decision-making. High rankings in searches and reviews? Mouthwatering photos on social media? Email promotions? Restaurants can create impact, from attracting new customers to keeping their current ones interested. In an ever-evolving and increasingly robust digital scene, the possibilities are endless.

147 "The Importance of a Digital Marketing Strategy in Today's World," Sacred Heart University, accessed June 1, 2020.

SUSTAINABILITY

FOOD WASTE

Sustainability takes different forms when it comes to the restaurant industry. Minimizing waste, using local ingredients, implementing environmentally friendly practices, increasing transparency, and creating shared value are only a few of many.

If we as individuals can contribute so much waste on our own, imagine a restaurant serving more people and dealing with more potential for waste in that process on a daily basis. No need to imagine—there's data. The Natural Resources Defense Council's report on waste brought to light that "U.S. restaurants (including full-service and quick-serve) are estimated to generate 22 billion to 33 billion pounds of food waste each year," responsible for about 18 percent of total food waste in the country.[148]

Expanding the scope of food waste beyond the kitchen is critical. There is space for food waste to occur at any point in this process, including farms, fishing practices, produce

---

148 Dana Gunders et al., "Wasted: How America is losing up to 40 Percent of its food from farm to fork," Natural Resources Defense Council, August 2017.

packing houses, manufacturing facilities, and transportation, even before it reaches the customer's table.[149]

One example is if perhaps fresh produce cannot reach a restaurant in time during the shipment process. Because fresh produce has a shorter shelf life, it is more likely to be discarded during that movement process. However, the standard USDA definition for food waste is in terms of what a consumer does not use fully, not taking into account any food wasted during the production and supply chain processes.

Waste can be broken down into three types of categories: pre-consumer waste, post-consumer waste, and disposables.[150]

Pre-consumer waste originates in the kitchen. Post-consumer waste is whatever is left on a customer's plate after they purchase a meal. Disposables are products, packaging, and utensils in restaurants.

PRE-CONSUMER WASTE

It's shocking to learn that "approximately 4 to 10 percent of food purchased by food service becomes pre-consumer waste," highlighting how much work needs to be done to decrease that jarring percentage.[151] The first way to reduce

149 "The Problem of Food Waste," FoodPrint, GRACE Communications Foundation, accessed June 1, 2020.

150 "Ways to Reduce Food Waste in Your Restaurant," WebstaurantStore, WebsaurantStore Food Service Equipment and Supply Company, August 6, 2018.

151 Dana Gunders et al., "Wasted: How America is losing up to 40 Percent of its food from farm to fork," Natural Resources Defense Council, August 2017.

pre-consumer waste is to make sure that ingredients are used to the fullest potential. This links to the idea of having food log systems (explained later) to keep track of information wasted because they help when figuring how much of each ingredient needs to be ordered so that the right amount can be used without surplus or slack.

Using ingredients to the fullest potential can also mean being resourceful. For example, scraps of vegetables can be thrown in a pot to make vegetable broth or some type of soup. "Nose to tail, root to stem—all of that is really just how you run a restaurant," is how Dan Barber, renowned chef and co-owner of Blue Hill, considers it—part of a larger framework.[152] What's great about this approach is that it minimizes the potential for waste and may in fact lead to creative problem-solving and new dishes. Another option is donating food (if allowed to redistribute), letting staff take it home, or giving it away for animal feed.

When I was in high school, I distinctly remember a kid bringing a large bag of bagels to our modern world history class (doesn't happen every day). He worked at a local bagel shop and brought all the bagels that didn't sell from the day before to school to share. It was good for us because we got free bagels (jalapeño is my favorite), a better option for the bagel shop since it wouldn't be dumping the bagels straight in the trash (though ideally it would use up inventory exactly to avoid handing extras out in the first place), and better for the environment because, again, they wouldn't be thrown away but rather consumed by hungry high schoolers.

---

152 Oliver Schwaner-Albright, "Five-Star Dining on Leftover Scraps?" *The Wall Street Journal*, June 22, 2015.

POST-CONSUMER WASTE

Post-consumer waste "makes up the vast majority of overall food losses in certain restaurant settings" and is "caused by excessive portion sizes and service methods such as all-you-can-eat buffets and free drink refills."[153]

One way restaurants fight this type of waste is to pay attention to portion size. The Cornell University Food and Brand Lab found that 55 percent of edible leftovers are left at a restaurant by customers.[154] A number of reasons could contribute to this, one of which is serving size. The standard serving sizes have increased dramatically over the past thirty years.[155] The bigger portions are not necessarily being eaten, which, of course, leads to food waste.

Restaurants might be wise to scale down different portions of food or make sure that an appropriate amount is served. Ensuring each portion is the same size when it comes out of the kitchen is also important because inconsistent portion sizes may make it difficult to keep a consistent amount of food waste tracked in logs. Another strategy is using logs to figure out what is left uneaten so that an appropriate amount of food is being ordered and only popular dishes make it on the menu. A common solution is offering to-go containers for customers to take any leftovers home to finish.

---

153 Dana Gunders et al., "Wasted: How America is losing up to 40 Percent of its food from farm to fork," Natural Resources Defense Council, August 2017.

154 "The Problem of Food Waste," FoodPrint, GRACE Communications Foundation, accessed June 1, 2020.

155 Ibid.

There are some questions about what can be redistributed regarding both pre-consumer and post-consumer waste, like unused ingredients or untouched buffet servings. Founder at Utah County Sustainability Coalition Sarah Bateman explained that for Utah in 2017, "If produce is whole or uncut, you can easily and legally donate it to food banks and shelters." But "once you cut into it or prepare it in any way, the rules change." But concerns are not limited to produce. Bateman highlights that "different countries, states, and counties might take slightly different approaches to food safety, preparation, and waste." Therefore, it is important for restaurants to conduct research and work off of appropriate laws and guidelines.[156] For example, all you can eat buffets are actually wasteful because the extra food that is left over, even if untouched, usually cannot be donated for health and safety reasons. In turn, a restaurant ends up having to throw it away. It is costly both financially and environmentally (double waste), so restaurants absolutely must be aware about areas of losses and reading up on necessary guidelines.[157]

DISPOSABLES

Lastly, disposables: using plastic boxes or utensils can be very detrimental to the environment, which is why it is worth looking at other options to reduce the reliance on such disposables. There are two prime ways to minimize disposable waste in restaurants. One way is to offer incentives to be more eco-friendly. Certain initiatives can help promote using

---

156 Anne Taylor, "Restaurants struggle with food donation laws," The Daily Universe, November 27, 2017.

157 "The Problem of Food Waste," FoodPrint, GRACE Communications Foundation, accessed June 1, 2020.

recyclable products as part of a business strategy in exchange for something else. For example, during Black Friday and Cyber Monday of 2019, Starbucks launched an incentive in which if a customer bought a sixteen-ounce refill tumbler for $40, they could bring it to participating Starbucks stores in January to get a free grande brewed coffee or grande hot tea.[158] This campaign helps minimize Starbucks's footprint and also earn money, even if only a little bit, simply by motivating the customers to buy a refillable tumbler. The act in turn enables a greener alternative to its regular packaging.

The second way is to actually change the packaging itself. Changing packaging is more expensive because it is used in daily operations, compared to the sporadic nature of incentives. A Technomic "Packaging Trends and Outlook" report found that 72 percent of customers assert that restaurants need to do more when it comes to being greener about packaging.[159] Yes, it's not cheap. Investing in biodegradable containers and recyclable alternatives may be initially expensive, but they are investments in helping the environment and connecting with consumers who are on the same page when it comes to taking initiative on the environmental front.

* * *

In addition, restaurants use analytics to aid in minimizing waste. The first order of business would be to conduct a food

---

158 "Black Friday and Cyber Monday: New gifts and deals coming to Starbucks," Starbucks Stories and News, Starbucks Corporation, November 19, 2019.

159 "Bowl over consumers with eco-friendly packaging," Restaurant Business, Restaurant Business Online, Winsight LLC., October 21, 2019.

waste audit.[160] A food waste audit tracks just how much food is being used, or in contrast, how much is not being used. It's about collecting data in usage over time so that restaurants can figure out the source of waste. There are two ways of going about conducting a food waste audit: a food log system and a traffic log system.[161]

A food log system is a running list that could be recorded either electronically or on paper about what is being discarded every day both in the kitchen and also of what customers leave on their plate. Over time, restaurants will be able to discern trends in what food is most likely to be wasted and in what quantities. This is essential information to figure out how to move forward to help reduce waste and save money.

A traffic log system records both the traffic of the restaurant and the weather for that day. Through this, restaurants will be able to figure out trends with customer volume during different times of the year. A traffic log system will help in providing the data to back up ordering decisions, like perhaps ordering less during times with low traffic and freezing weather and more with high traffic and pleasant weather. What's helpful about this log system is that the POS systems we discussed earlier in this book have these capabilities in the technology, so tracking trends and mapping out the future with past data are easier.

---

160 "Ways to Reduce Food Waste in Your Restaurant," WebstaurantStore, WebsaurantStore Food Service Equipment and Supply Company, August 6, 2018.

161 Ibid.

Ultimately, focusing on minimizing waste does a number of things. It helps restaurants be cognizant of their impacts on the environment from the very start of their supply chain, ensures that inventory is being used adequately when in the restaurant to minimize losses, and has the power to attract customers who are also interested in being part of green initiatives. Taking advantage of analytics and identifying different sources of waste can help restaurants do their part to keep as efficient as they are environmentally conscious.

CHAPTER 12

LOCAL SOURCING

———

Growing up, my family and I would grow a variety of herbs and vegetables in our backyard. Mint, curry leaves, basil, cilantro, jalapeños, squash, eggplant, tomatoes—you name it. It was pleasing to know that it was all natural, and not to mention, satisfyingly fresh and flavorful. As a side note, one tip about growing mint (learned through experience) is to make sure that it is contained. Otherwise, if given enough space and water, it will grow wildly in your backyard and onto your neighbor's lawn and will continue to conquer territory far and wide like an ancient emperor discovering new land. Mint for days. Applying the concept of going and growing local to a larger context helps plant the seeds of transparency, menu mobility, and freshness for restaurants today.

Locally sourced ingredients matter to customers, otherwise known as the farm-to-table movement.[162] About 80 percent of "table-service restaurant operators, and a similar proportion of fast-casual operators, report that consumer interest in locally

———

162 Lorri Mealy, "Local Food trends for Restaurants," The Balance Small Business, Dotdash, January 18, 2020.

sourced foods has grown in the past two years," prompting shifts in menu and sourcing.[163] One type of local sourcing is with hyperlocal foods, or ingredients grown in house, like an herb garden in the physical restaurant space. Hyperlocal sourcing made the National Restaurant Association's 2019 list of top ten culinary trends, ranging from on-site beer brewing to house-made items.[164]

Restaurants that source hyperlocally are gaining traction. A great example is Uncommon Ground in Chicago, Illinois. It's not only the state's first certified organic brewery but also the first certified organic rooftop farm in the United States.[165] The restaurant uses earthboxes to ensure that nutrients are evenly distributed among plants, beehives for pollination and honey, and planter boxes to grow a variety of plants. What's interesting about Uncommon Ground is that it goes beyond the food when it comes to sustainability: the deck was created from recycled materials, the soil is organic, and it implements a comprehensive irrigation design to ensure optimal water use.[166] The farm grows produce used in both of its locations: delicious, nutritious, and fresh.

With hyperlocal food, it's convenient for chefs to grab the day's ingredient inventory in the restaurant itself, though it takes time, skill, and money to tend properly. Therefore, sourcing fresh ingredients from the local area is a broader

---

163 "The State of Restaurant Sustainability 2018," National Restaurant Association, accessed June 1, 2020.

164 "What's Hot: 2019 Culinary Forecast," National Restaurant Association, accessed June 1, 2020.

165 "Organic Rooftop Farm," Uncommon Ground, accessed June 1, 2020.

166 Ibid.

implementation of this growing trend, supporting the community in exchange for a delicious harvest.

Sourcing locally provides numerous benefits, like stimulating the local economy, helping the environment, greater and fresher options, and more.[167] For one, it's important to look at the supply chain in a more humanized way. Sourcing locally does this since it focuses on the relationship aspect and can take form in different ways, including buying through farmers markets or farmers themselves and buying a community supported agriculture (CSA) box.

Haven't heard of a CSA box before? Dana Angelo White, a registered dietitian, explained what CSA programs are all about, for both every day and wholesale customers:[168]

> "By joining a CSA, members basically buy a portion (or share) of a local farm's harvest for the year. You pay an initial fee in exchange for a weekly box of fresh and seasonal items. Some CSA programs also offer members the chance to work off their share by helping out on the farm. You might pick up your goodies at the farm or a designated pick-up spot (some CSAs even offer home delivery)."

White went on to explain what one receives:

> "[A] share will vary depending on the specific farm, but offerings typically include fruit and

---

167 "The Pro's and Cons of Local Sourcing," Chartered Institute of Procurement & Supply, accessed June 1, 2020.

168 Dana Angelo White, "Is it Worth it to Join a CSA?" Food Network, Television Food Network, April 2009.

vegetables as well as baked goods, dairy and eggs—
even honey and flowers may be available. My CSA
offers a choice of fruits, vegetables, flowers, or a
combination of the three. Of course, the variety
depends on the seasonality; as it becomes available on the farm, it will show up in your CSA box."

A CSA box is just one example of local sourcing, though it is
more variable than simply buying through a farmers market
itself. Doing so brings profit for local farmers and producers
involved in the supply chain, generating business that helps the
area. CSAs are helpful beyond a business standpoint. "Farmer's
markets, CSAs, and community gardens generate important
non-economic benefits to their communities" like the "prolif-
eration of social interactions" or "helping empower individuals
to become managers and leaders within their communities."[169]
By investing in various methods of local sourcing, restaurants
can keep them powered as valuable centers in a community,
be they economic, social, or skill-building.

* * *

When it comes to the environment, local sourcing has an
impact. "Food miles" is a term often used to describe the distance of food being transported. Sourcing locally reduces such
"food miles," so the shorter the time food travels, the less carbon
emissions and waste involved in the transportation process.[170]

---

169 Rebecca Dunning, "Research-Based Support and Extension Outreach
for Local Food Systems," Center for Environmental Farming Systems,
November 2011.

170 Jennifer Reynolds, "What Is Behind The Trend Of Local Food?" Food
Secure Canada, Winter 2016.

NPR Chief Business Editor Pallavi Gogoi noted that "consumers who have been educated by movies like *An Inconvenient Truth* now pore over 'food miles' and 'carbon footprints.' The message seems to be: if you buy organic, you care about your own body; if you buy local, you care about your body and the environment."[171] Looking at our actions, as a consumer or a producer in the context of the environment and health, has already taken shape now, though there is still a ways to go.

Besides helping the environment, buying local ensures freshness. Because it takes less time for ingredients to be transported because they are harvested so close, restaurants have access to ingredients more quickly, ensuring they stay fresh. For example, if you ever go to your regular, chain grocery store, you will sometimes find that fruits and vegetables look suspiciously identical in nature or beaten up from the shipment process (often hidden at the bottom of the pile—we know your secrets, grocery stores). Contrast this to your local farmers market, where produce is often plucked and in your hands much faster, evidenced by its freshness and taste.

I remember going on road trips with my family in Texas during the summer and stopping in a small town called Frederick. There were small farmers markets near the road, so we were always compelled to stop and buy ourselves deliciously ripe and juicy peaches. There's nothing like eating a good peach when it's in season, I'll tell you that. Sourcing local ensures a higher degree of freshness delivered quickly, something chefs will appreciate in preparation and customers will enjoy in taste

---

171 Cinnamon Janzer, "The History of the Farm to Table Movement," Upserve, Upserve, Inc., June 22, 2018.

and transparency. Another perk of the shorter supply chain is that restaurants have access to more variety from producers since they know food will stay fresh in the short distance traveled. This is great for restaurants to expand menu options with more variety and also experiment seasonally.[172]

The USDA has an interesting "Seasonal Produce Guide" to give restaurant owners and chefs in the United States an idea of when fruit and vegetables are typically at their peak and thus when to incorporate it in the menu on a seasonal basis.[173] Even as a consumer, it's helpful to know what's in season, and also worth noting that they typically cost less when they are. Local sourcing enables restaurants to maximize when produce is at its best, syncing a menu with agricultural patterns to keep it fresh and exciting.

The next time you visit a restaurant, see if they have a seasonal menu based on local ingredients. Grand Central Bakery in Portland and Seattle puts immense care in its ingredients, the treatment of employees, and the welfare of local communities. It's one of many restaurants that mixes up menu items seasonally as a product of sourcing locally. As its website states, "because we know fresh, local ingredients just taste better, we use a wide variety of local products in our cooking and baking that reflect the best of the season."[174] They share that "our salad greens come from local farms for as many months of the year as they're available," highlighting the variable nature of the menu,

---

172 "Sourcing Locally for Restaurants," San Diego Farmer Bureau, accessed June 1, 2020.

173 "Seasonal Produce Guide," U.S. Department of Agriculture, accessed June 1, 2020.

174 "Menus," Grand Central Bakery, accessed June 1, 2020.

as well as its importance to the restaurant's mission.[175] Grand Central Bakery works to "be part of a robust local economy and support a sustainable regional food system," and partnering locally is just one of many impactful ways to do that.[176]

While local sourcing does interest customers, there are still plenty of restaurants that do not harvest ingredients locally. Why? A number of barriers exist that prevent local sourcing from being a successful reality for every single food and beverage institution, such as risks or costs.

Professor John Quelch from Harvard Business School and Harvard's T.H. Chan School of Public Health explained the complications of local sourcing:

> "…local sourcing adds complexity, increases risk and fragments the supply chain. Even if you have a standard quality control procedure for all of your sources, you're not going to be able to monitor them on-site at every location. You're going to have to put your trust in the suppliers to live up to the expectations laid down in the quality control guidelines."[177]

So a shorter supply chain is not necessarily a simpler one. Restaurants must oversee each step of the process to ensure

---

175 Ibid.

176 "About," Grand Central Bakery, accessed June 1, 2020.

177 Nicole Torres, "Why Sourcing Local Food Is So Hard for Restaurants," *Harvard Business Review,* June 15, 2016.

that it meets standards, especially if restaurants hold themselves to sustainable practices.

Price is also a contention, since locally sourced ingredients can lead to higher-priced menu items and a loss if there is not the demand to compensate. Even if "interested consumers expect to pay higher prices for the locally sourced, farm-to-table product," the fact is that "many consumers are price sensitive, and they are looking for safe food at a reasonable price."[178] Despite this, "the more people who have the disposable income to be able to pay the price differential, and the more informed consumers become, the more that trend will grow," Quelch affirmed.[179] It's a community and financial investment in many ways.

Keeping this trend in mind going forward is helpful for restaurants to build connections with the local community, reap the benefits of a shorter supply chain with freshness and options, reduce impact on the environment, and generate profit with transparency and emphasis on natural ingredients. These are tremendous benefits. While going local is not always easy, it may prove rather fruitful in the long term, thanks to trends highlighting increased customer interest and emphasis on sustainable practices.

---

178 Ibid.

179 Ibid.

CHAPTER 13

CREATING SHARED VALUE

With the help of professional responsibility and business ethics courses, many undergraduate business schools today prompt students to think about business as something multifaceted, something more than companies bringing in cash day in and day out. Generating profit is important, yes, but not the only aspect of business to zero in on. It's essential to think about stakeholders, issues, and additional factors involved when making business decisions, as it comes with impacts, be they environmental, economic, or social.

The Gies College of Business at the University of Illinois at Urbana-Champaign makes teaching students this and more a priority in their "Professional Responsibility and Business" (BUS 101) course for first-years. I took this class and a subsequent, more in-depth class called "Principles of Professional Responsibility" (BUS 302) my freshman year of college. These courses helped lay the foundation to looking at business through a kaleidoscope of factors necessary to informing future professionals and leaders in business. A key concept I learned and further explored is called "creating shared value."

Creating shared value is a term coined by the Harvard Business School's Michael Porter and Mark Kramer in their "Creating Shared Value" publication in *Harvard Business Review*.[180] Creating shared value is the practice of adding value, whether it be social or economic, in the process of making profit. In other words, the power to uplift is ingrained in a company's operations to fiscal success. Hence, the fact that adding value is part of core strategy makes it fundamentally different from philanthropy or corporate social responsibility, as described by Porter and Kramer. Adding value is not external to the business but what keeps it successful.

Branding strategy has a way of connecting itself to sustainability through the practice of creating shared value, as we'll see in the upcoming Shake Shack example. Shake Shack connects fine-casual dining to sustainability and to creating shared value with its business model.

When he opened a hot dog cart in Madison Square Park, Danny Meyer's original goal was to help support an art exhibit.[181] But what he didn't know was that this unassuming pop-up, after three summers of operation in the New York heat, would experience tremendous success. Who knew this would be the humble beginnings of the popular American

---

180 Michael E. Porter and Mark R. Kramer, "Creating Shared Value," *Harvard Business Review*, August 25, 2015.

181 "Grill & Chill this Summer with Recipes for our Flat-Top Dogs, Revealed in "Shake Shack: Recipes & Stories," Shake Shack, April 28, 2017.

chain Shake Shack? All thanks to hot dogs and supporting the arts.

Because of his ambitious pursuits in the food industry since then, Meyer currently oversees many restaurants as an esteemed New York City restaurateur and current CEO of Union Square Hospitality Group.[182] One of his notable accomplishments is founding Shake Shack in 2004 from the hot dog cart. Shake Shack is an American "fine-casual dining" establishment that specializes in a range of burgers and milkshakes. Since its opening, Shake Shack has continued its operations in over 235 locations in fifteen countries, a number that continues to grow. Hot dog!

But it seems like there is an endless supply of burger and milkshake places vying to satisfy customers at any given time. So what makes this particular chain different?

I read up on Shake Shack's Form 10-K (for the fiscal year ending December 2018), which was actually pretty interesting once you accept how tiny the font is. Form 10-K, required by the US Securities and Exchange Commission for publicly traded companies, gives a summary of a company's performance with financial statements and important operational information.[183]

The document emphasized the company's "marketing efforts focus on interacting with our guests in an authentic,

---

182 "Danny Meyer," Union Square Hospitality Group, accessed June 1, 2020.

183 "Form 10-K," U.S. Securities and Exchange Commission, accessed June 1, 2020.

innovative manner which creates memorable, meaningful experiences. The experience that we provide for our guests and local communities has generated a growing loyal following that promotes our brand through word-of-mouth."[184]

As the Form 10-K hinted at, CEO of Shake Shack Randy Garutti, who runs under Meyer's Union Square Hospitality Group, said that the chain does little advertising and marketing.[185] Instead, it pushes the concept of fine-casual dining both nationally and internationally, aiming to establish a presence for itself in terms of quality and experience. It's not about flashy posters or ads that Shake Shack is trying to push out to market itself. The burger chain focuses on the value of the product and service, a different strategy.

Garutti conceded that Shake Shack won't be the last to make a great burger.[186] There are indeed an endless number of places to buy a delicious burger. But with the following, interest, and branding they have cultivated until today, Shake Shack is certainly not going anywhere anytime soon.

The success of Shake Shack rests on one key equation, according to Meyer: high-quality ingredients + accessibility + affordability = fine-casual dining.

In a TEDx Talk, Meyer discussed the appeals of branding Shake Shack as a combination of both fast-food and

---

184 United States Securities and Exchange Commission, *Form 10-K Shake Shack Inc.* (2018).

185 "Watch CNBC's full interview with Shake Shack's CEO Randy Garutti," *CNBC*, June 21, 2019. video, 8:07.

186 Ibid.

fine-dining concept.[187] Fast food requires immediate preparation and service of food (be it drive-through, takeout, or sit-down) and is often sought for its convenience and cheap prices. Fine dining is more of a sit-down style, in which food, service, and atmosphere are held to a high standard, associated with a higher price. Combining these concepts together creates a largely unexplored territory that Meyer taps into (and will continue to trend): the fantastic world of fast-casual.

With the blended characteristics of fine dining and fast food, Meyer asserts that "you can get the exact same quality food [as fine dining] much more accessible… and create the kind of systems around that good taste that allow it to be a chain."[188] He attributes the fine-dining aspect of the chain to the food: natural ingredients and high quality that are on par with those of finer establishments. The "casual" part of the mix is seen in the accessibility and affordability of the food, something Meyer finds contributes to the chain's success. After all, who wouldn't want a great meal with quality service and affordable pricing? In the Form 10-K, the company emphasized that "we embrace our fine-dining heritage and are committed to sourcing premium, sustainable ingredients, such as all-natural, hormone and antibiotic-free beef, chicken, and pork, while offering excellent value to our guests."[189] Fine-casual dining is rooted in sustainability. It's part of the Shake Shack identity.

---

187 *TEDx Talks*, "The Convergence of Casual and Fine | Danny Meyer | TEDx Manhattan," March 20, 2015, video, 17:36.

188 Ibid.

189 United States Securities and Exchange Commission, *Form 10-K Shake Shack Inc.* (2018).

Shake Shack is not alone in the emerging service structure of fine-casual dining. According to Darren Tristano, president of food industry research and consulting firm Technomic, the concept of fine-casual dining is gaining traction as "creative chefs—the ones who would have typically gone for a forty-seat fine-dining restaurant—launch fine fast-casual concepts because they can see the great growth potential."[190] Converting that potential into measurable success, Shake Shack's emphasis on the fusion of two seemingly different dining categories sets it apart from traditional burger and milkshake institutions. High-caliber food at an affordable price grants greater access to more people of all walks of life. And as Meyer mentioned, Shake Shack puts in the framework for those variables to thrive and take the chain to the next level.

So how does this all relate to this chapter about sustainability? Why are we talking about branding? You'll find that it is all very interconnected. It's this strategy of only using high-quality and fresh ingredients as part of the fine-casual dining equation that allows Shake Shack to deliver something more than a good burger: a good business model for the community as well.

While accessibility and affordability are important to the fine-casual dining equation, high-quality, locally sourced ingredients are absolutely essential to it. Let's take a look into specifics when it comes to Shake Shack sourcing and its relationship to others. Considering the roadblocks that come from expanding internationally when it comes to

---

190 David Farkas, "Fine Dining Takes On Fast Casual," US Foods, US Foods Inc., accessed June 1, 2020.

supplies, Garutti explained that "on-the-ground sourcing" is a solution that not only allows Shake Shack to have access to local vendors and thus fresh ingredients, but also foster a connection with the community.[191] Working local vendors into Shake Shack's supply chain allows it to stimulate the economic growth in a particular area while also tending to the chain's own goals of preparing its menu items with only the best ingredients. Incorporating the local community is part of Shake Shack's operations.

This circles back to the idea of creating shared value. By bringing in a local element, Shake Shack is able to be sustainable in a way that brings the restaurant the freshest produce and creates movement in local economies. It's a win-win situation that uplifts the community, encourages sustainability, and brings in profit. It's interesting to see how the implementation of a concept like fine-casual dining lends itself to sustainable practices in this example.

Mastering the art of the fine-casual dining equation is not the only way Shake Shack appeals to customers, but to understate it would be to ignore the impact of its philosophy on business operations. Utilizing effective and value-adding supply chains, catering to a larger audience, and offering competitive prices help Shake Shack not only thrive, but (milk)shake up the status quo for fast food and fine dining for the future.

Creating shared value is no easy task, however. Brandon Tidwell, the former manager of sustainability for Darden

---

191 Danielle Wiener-Bronner, "Inside Shake Shack's unusual global strategy," *CNN*, June 18, 2019.

Restaurants, wrote that "making shared value a core part of every business decision takes time and a commitment to understanding the full impact of one's operations."[192] That's why Darden found that "by working collaboratively with other businesses and our full value chain, we can accomplish more than what we could do alone."[193] In other words, taking actionable steps to create long-term impact, like helping solve issues through partnerships, is a way to pave the road to more sustainable operations. By creating shared value, restaurants can profit by being sustainable, since both are integrated in the business model itself. Intertwined for impact.

192 Brandon Tidwell, "Creating Shared Value," *Darden Digest (Blog), Darden Concepts, Inc.,* October 10, 2013.

193 Ibid.

FOOD CHOICE

MENU OPTIONS

"Effective menus are critical to the financial health of a foodservice operation and serve as a "driver" of the business," wrote Pennsylvania State University's professor Beth Egan in her textbook, *Introduction to Food Production and Service*.[194] Menus matter to drive profit but are also subject to change. Being aware of the changes helps restaurant owners tailor their menus to better cater to different needs and preferences over time.[195] In particular, the trends toward shorter menus, diverse options, convenience items, and unexplored cuisines and flavors contribute to the evolution of menu choices accessible to customers today.

SHORTER MENUS

Instead of offering menus that are long and contain abundance of different items, there's a new trend now: shorter menus.[196] Shorter menus allow for ease in ordering and in

---

194 Beth Egan, "Chapter 4 - Menus," Introduction to Food Production and Service, PennState, accessed June 1, 2020.

195 Ibid.

196 Julie Littman and Emma Liem Beckett, "5 restaurant trends that will define 2020," Restaurant Dive, Industry Dive, accessed June 1, 2020.

operations that longer menus simply cannot match. The benefit of a shorter menu is that because there are less items, it takes a shorter amount of time for guests to decide. A Bournemouth University study found that "in fast food restaurants, customers wanted to pick from six items per category. In fine dining establishments, they preferred a little more choice – between seven and ten items," highlighting the idea that less is more to prevent the customer from feeling overwhelmed.[197]

Psychologically, this strategy is good because it reduces cognitive dissonance after making a purchase.

Cognitive dissonance in the marketing context is the conflict customers experience when having feelings of regret after making a purchasing decision, dubbed buyer's remorse. How many times have you picked something from a menu and then had second thoughts about it?

For example, I remember going to a Chinese restaurant where the menu was almost ten pages long. Trying to figure out what I should order, I spent so much time analyzing the different menu options, flipping pages restlessly to find the "perfect" dish. I'm the type to do ample research before I choose something, but how can you conduct proper research on over fifty menu items? After I gave my order to the waiter, I wondered if I should have opted for something else. Would that have made me happier? Who knows? Large menus easily evoke this feeling since the number of options to choose from often causes customers to brew conflicted feelings about what they should order. Therefore, shorter menus decrease

---

197 Richard Gray, "The secret tricks hidden inside restaurant menus," *BBC*, November 20, 2017.

the chance of buyer's remorse, make it easier for customers to order, and thus increase the likelihood of customer satisfaction with selections compared to their experience using longer menus.

A smaller menu doesn't limit creative or new options or cause guests to become tired of the same offerings. Interestingly enough, it actually means more flexibility, since menu items can be swapped around according to season and popularity, and won't impose a toll on inventory and employee training. Fred LeFranc, managing partner at Results Thru Strategy, explains that "if you streamline your menu, you can do so much more to improve your efficiencies, the quality of the product, the order time for the customers."[198] This contrasts with offering fifty different dishes at once, since ingredients respective to those dishes must be stocked at all time in case ordered and employees must be trained in how to prepare each item. Tim Fenton, previously McDonald's chief operating officer, echoed this idea, asserting that "we need to do fewer products with better execution" to let the restaurant "breathe."[199]

An example of a streamlined menu is the popular and ever-expanding chain In-N-Out Burger. Their menu is famously simple: double-double, cheeseburger, hamburger, French fries, beverages, and shakes. Not only does it make it easy for customers to order, but it also make easier for employees to efficiently construct and customize menu items, reducing labor training.[200]

---

198 Jonathan Lister, "What is Dissonance in Marketing?" Chron, Hearst Newspapers, LLC, accessed June 1, 2020.

199 Roberto Ferdman, "Americans are tired of long restaurant menus," *The Washington Post*, September 18, 2014.

200 Julie Littman and Emma Liem Beckett, "5 restaurant trends that will define 2020," Restaurant Dive, Industry Dive, accessed June 1, 2020.

PLANT-BASED, VEGETARIAN, AND VEGAN OPTIONS

The next trend expands the menu to invite more meatless options. Billy Roberts, a senior food and drink analyst at Mintel, noted that "Americans are more and more avoiding food products with artificial ingredients and GMOs, and vegetarian, vegan, and free-from foods have grown to be regarded as healthier options." Roberts went on to write that though health incentives affect decision-making, "taste is the driving force behind purchase and eating decisions" when it comes to plant-based options. Consumer interest toward plant-based proteins stems (no pun intended) mainly from taste and health consciousness, according to a Mintel study of why US adults choose such options. Environmental impact (13 percent) still plays a role but is not as much of a reason as taste (52 percent) and health (39 percent).[201] Therefore, when including plant-based menu items, taste should not be overlooked.

"Fifty-eight of the biggest U.S. restaurant chains boasted at least one plant-based dish on the menu last year, up from fifty-five in 2018, according to an annual survey by the Good Food Institute," a trend that continues to grow.[202] Chains like Carl's Jr. are implementing Beyond Meat options to diversify their menu offerings and attract customers based on dietary restrictions, lifestyle, health consciousness, environmental impacts, animal impacts, or simply curiosity.

What's interesting is that this demand is not only in physical locations, but in online ordering as well. "Vegan and

---

201 "Taste Is The Top Reason Us Consumers Eat Plant-based Proteins," Mintel, Mintel Group Ltd, February 15, 2018.

202 Janet Forgrieve, "U.S. Restaurant Chains Make Plant-Based Options To Fit Their Brands," Forbes, Forbes Media LLC., February 29, 2020.

vegetarian dishes claimed seven of Grubhub's top ten spots, compared to just three last year. Further, vegan orders rose 27 percent in popularity overall this year versus 2018."[203] The trend toward such options doesn't stop at Grubhub. Postmates described 2019 as "the year for plant-based 'meat,'" with 385,589 plant-based protein options ordered.[204] And with increased implementation of plant-based meat options, this trend is only going to grow.

A 2019 *Forbes* article brings attention to the website Happy-Cow, "which works like Yelp, but for vegan and vegetarian food" and "lists over 24,000 veg-friendly eateries in the United States, including 1,474 exclusively vegan restaurants."[205] I checked HappyCow's listings about ten months after the article was published, and now there are over 27,580 veg-friendly listings and 1,641 vegan restaurants, an increase for both figures.[206] So much growth in less than a year! The top states with the most veg-friendly listings (which includes vegan, vegetarian, veg-options, and chains) on HappyCow include California (4,411 locations), New York (2,099), Florida (2,005), and Texas (1,552)—all over the nation.

My older brother, a 2020 University of California, Berkeley graduate, is no stranger to California's dynamic restaurant scene and

203 Alicia Kelso, "The Foods You'll Be Ordering In 2020, According To Postmates, Grubhub, Uber Eats And DoorDash," Forbes, Forbes Media LLC., December 10, 2019.

204 "A Year in Postmates: What We Ordered 2019," Postmates, *Medium,* December 9, 2019.

205 Brian Kateman, "Vegan Restaurants Are On The Rise," Forbes, Forbes Media LLC., August 21, 2019.

206 "Vegan & Vegetarian Restaurants in USA," HappyCow Healthy Eating Guide, accessed June 1, 2020.

its adventurous population of customers. I asked him about his experiences eating out, and he shared "the Bay Area is one of the more progressive areas" when it comes to food. He mentioned that "now, there's a lot of restaurants catering to vegans and vegetarians in the area, especially in Berkeley and North Oakland. Those cities are known for a very thriving restaurant scene."

He discussed one location in particular that highlighted the diversity of those options. "There's a restaurant called Souley Vegan in Oakland. They specialize in vegan and plant-based Soul food," he shared. "It's something I've never had anywhere else in all the places I've been in the United States." Souley Vegan has its own 100 percent plant-based adaptations of classic Southern foods, like chicken and waffles or calamari. In the eatery, it's seitan "chicken" and waffles while "calamari" is created with fried hearts of palm—creative, meatless alternatives that still bring forth iconic Southern flavors. Yum. He revealed that there was much demand for it as "there's always a big line when we head down there. It's very popular, especially among college students and the locals."

I looked up Souley Vegan and learned that it was founded in 2006 by chef and owner Tamearra Dyson.[207] It has been featured in various food websites and even visited by Food Network's pride and joy Guy Fieri on his legendary show *Diners, Drive-Ins, and Dives*. I'm guilty of watching one too many episodes of that show. But offering tasty food choices that integrate Southern staples and plant-based dining showcases how Souley Vegan caters to vegans, vegetarians, and motivates even the most meat-loving customers to branch out and give it a try.

---

207 "Press," Souley Vegan, accessed June 1, 2020.

CONVENIENCE ITEMS

Grab-and-go options are becoming more prominent as customers prioritize convenience. The number of restaurants offering items to quickly grab on the way to work or school is only going to grow. Marketing specialist Hiba Amin shared that "smart restaurant owners would be wise to pay attention to this trend and offer similar options for guests alongside the traditional model, without compromising their unique brand."[208] This could take form in offering menu favorites as grab-and-go options, ensuring that quality remains the same.

Another form of convenience items are at-home meals or kits. Emma Liem Beckett discussed this trend in her article "6 restaurant trends that could turn tables in 2019." "According to NPD Group, one of the biggest menu demands that have been shaping the marketplace of late is interest in blended, eat-at-home meals."[209] Beckett proposed that "restaurants can cash in on this trend by offering packaged prepared foods meant for takeaway alongside their made-to-order menu items, a strategy chains such as Starbucks have doubled down on in recent years." This area is key in exploring, especially if the restaurant's target market would benefit from expanded convenience.

GLOBAL FLAVORS

The desire to experience different cuisines and international flavors is ablaze in the restaurant industry. Customers are looking to try new dishes to literally get a taste of another

---

208 Hiba Amin, "10 Trends Shaping the Restaurant Industry in 2019," ChefHero, March 21, 2019.

209 Emma Liem Beckett, "6 restaurant trends that could turn tables in 2019," Restaurant Dive, Industry Dive, January 7, 2019.

part of the world, an experimental desire not as pronounced a decade ago. But keep in mind the generation behind it. According to research from Mintel, "Gen Z consumers are driving consumption of more emerging international food and drink," including Indian, Middle Eastern, and African that are less common than Italian, Mexican, and Chinese in the United States.[210] This is critical information, as understanding one's target market better helps restaurants tailor menu offerings to best suit their customers' wants and needs. I personally love to experience different types of cuisine, from Uzbek to Uyghur, actively seeking new places to try out. Offering options that explore these cuisines and deviate from familiarity will help restaurants separate themselves from a sea of comfort food and otherwise well-known cuisines, attracting namely Gen Z, followed by millennial, and later Gen X, customers. It's time to spice things up.

An unfinished essay is often called a "living document" or "work in progress" since it's bound to be changed again at some point. A menu is similar. With customer preferences shifting with time, competitive restaurants take this into account to offer what the customer wants. Of course, while staying true to their own identity and message. You'll soon learn that with the help of structured experimenting, restaurants can test the waters to adapt their offerings and provide menu options both in demand and to brand.

---

210 "IFT18: Generation Z Set To Impact The Future Of Food And Drink Innovation," Mintel, Mintel Group Ltd, July 16, 2018.

CHAPTER 15

EXPERIMENTING

If now's the time to try anything in food, it's time to experiment. It doesn't have to be with liquid nitrogen like ambitious chefs on TV, but rather with offering something innovative to the customer that piques interest. Taco Bell is a fun place to start, a fantastic role model for pushing out innovative creations time after time.

At one point in Taco Bell history, the fast-food chain challenged itself with a mission: offer a unique twist on standard fries. Taco Bell had tried it before, but no previous version was ever truly successful. Its ultimate goal was to turn "classic Mexican foods" into something new and exciting, while keeping true to its brand. With this in mind, Liz Matthews, Taco Bell's global food innovation officer, and her team got to work. Taco Bell tested fries and experimented with all sorts of flavors to perfect the revolutionized fry. Trial after trial, flavor after flavor, the team relentlessly worked to discover the magic formula. And they did.

Matthews and her team were responsible for inventing the award-winning $1 Nacho Fries, a menu item Taco Bell lovers are no stranger to. It performed astoundingly well as soon as it hit the market. In fact, "In the first five weeks, restaurants sold more than 53 million orders. One out of every three orders included fries."[211] With hard work, persistence, and trials, you can Taco-Bellieve that people were hooked on Nacho Fries. To stress just how wildly successful they were (if 53 million orders were not enough), "Nacho Fries broke new product records and won NRN's coveted MenuMasters award in 2019 for Best New Item," Nation's Restaurant News reported.[212] Taco Bell now uses the legendary Nacho Fries as a powerful limited-time offer to "inspire other items," opening the door for future innovations.

Of course, not all restaurants have the budget, team, and resources for testing like Taco Bell, to work on crafting the perfect menu items through trial after trial of calculated experimenting. Restaurants can look to Taco Bell's example as inspiration to try out new culinary pursuits and encourage menu innovation. Why?

Shannon Cushen, the director of marketing for Fuchs North America, revealed that "consumers, specifically millennials and Gen Z, get bored incredibly easy these days" and "are always seeking out new and different flavors and taste sensations."[213] Serving the same thing, even if good, can come

---

211 Nancy Luna, "MenuMasters 2019: Best New Item," Nation's Restaurant News, Informa USA, Inc., March 27, 2019.

212 Nancy Luna, "Taco Bell's global chief food innovation officer Liz Matthews develops inventive menu items," Nation's Restaurant News, Informa USA, Inc., January 22, 2020.

213 Kelly Hensel, "2020 Flavor Forecast," *Food Technology Magazine* 73, no. 12 (December 1, 2019).

across as uninspiring or stale. With changing preferences, customers look for something more, something different.

Areas to experiment include seasonal items and food trends described in earlier chapters. Using menu engineering (covered soon) is helpful to assess the impact of new products if testing for the long term. It doesn't mean that new items will be a hit once implemented, but even in failures and slow sales, restaurants can still pick up and learn what sticks and what doesn't. Otherwise, restaurants should look toward guidelines to figure out what products have potential to perform.

A *Harvard Business Review* article offers guidelines for launching new products, not limited to a certain industry but helpful for larger companies as well.[214]

First, set up clear measures for data to identify what would mean success and what would constitute a failure. Second, launch the product in random markets to avoid bias. Third, track effectiveness of the new product and its impact on other products sold. Does it potentially crowd out other items? And lastly, interpret reasons for the success or failure of the product for a holistic picture of its impact.

While originally intended for larger companies to implement in a random market, small businesses can apply this same testing framework to an extent to analyze how new products are helping or potentially hurting the business at a smaller scale. Asking these questions is helpful before launching a

---

214 Jeff Fossett, Duncan Gilchrist, and Michael Luca, "Using Experiments to Launch New Products," *Harvard Business Review*, November 5, 2018.

new menu item. Simply throwing something new on the menu can turn out to be costly and wasteful if there isn't demand.

* * *

In figuring out what menu items restaurants should carry and incorporating trends in customer preferences, many businesses use data analysis. Collecting customer data "helps restaurants figure out what exactly customers want and how they can create new dishes or tweak existing ones, and how to better tailor their marketing to individual customers, all with the ultimate goal of boosting sales." Restaurants can gain access to this data through customers' signing up for loyalty programs, expressing opinions over review platforms like Yelp, filling out a survey for a reward, submitting personal information to gain access to Wi-Fi, and more.[215]

There are three main benefits of using predictive analytics (such as POS systems) in the restaurant space.[216] First is improving accuracy of orders. POS systems track when items are ordered, allowing for restaurants to prepare for demand with a stocked inventory. The second is forecasting trends by analyzing data from the past. This is helpful in analyzing seasonal shifts to curate new menu changes according to these changes. The third benefit is that it saves money by reducing food waste. Using proper analytics, restaurants can learn what inventory is being used and how much. They

---

215 Whitney Filloon, "Why Restaurants are So Hungry for Your Personal Data," Eater, Vox Media, LLC., October 10, 2018.

216 Ryan Andrews, "How Restaurants Are Using Data and Analytics to Increase Profits," Eat, July 17, 2019.

can thus take action to create a menu that maximizes profit and minimizes expenses.

A more comprehensive way to analyze customer data in relation to the restaurant as a whole is through menu engineering. Menu engineering "is an empirical way to evaluate restaurant menu pricing, using your restaurant data to influence your menu's design and content decisions."[217] To help evaluate and curate a more effective menu, "it involves categorizing all menu items into one of four menu engineering categories, based on the profitability and popularity of each item."[218]

Investing in POS systems like Eat or Toast is helpful since they offer data on food costs and menu item prices. Otherwise, manually completing formulas is necessary to identify strong and weak parts of the menu, a tedious but highly informative task. Menu engineering is a process that takes time since it requires many calculations and comparative analyses. However, conducting this analysis monthly, seasonally, or semiannually is helpful in finding what the least and most unpopular dishes are and can increase profits over 15 percent.[219]

With its widespread use, there are helpful templates online to assist restaurants in recording information and interpreting what it means. The menu has more impact on a customer than you'd think, from selection and pricing to design and phrasing. For example, a 2017 Stanford study "found that vegetables that

217 Allie Van Duyne, "How to Make Your Menu a Money-Maker," Toast, Toast, Inc., accessed June 1, 2020.

218 Ibid.

219 "Restaurant Menu Engineering: Increasing Profits," RestoHub, Touch Bistro Inc., accessed June 1, 2020.

have been given indulgent-sounding descriptions – such as 'dynamite chili', 'sweet sizzling green beans', and 'crispy shallots' – on a cafeteria menu were picked 23 percent more often because it made them sound more exciting and flavoursome."[220] The study recommends that "this novel, low-cost intervention could easily be implemented in cafeterias, restaurants, and consumer products to increase selection of healthier options."[221]

I find this example particularly interesting because menu engineering is used in a way that promotes a healthy lifestyle, relabeling vegetables to appeal to customers. Menu engineering can be used to push all sorts of items, healthy or not. Imagine a restaurant featuring a "decadent, warm triple-chocolate cake topped generously with our world-famous hot fudge." Sounds more tempting than simply slapping "chocolate cake" on a menu. Now I want a slice! Menu engineering can be used expertly to encourage customers toward certain items. The parts of a menu that you previously glossed over before, menu engineers will tell you have a distinct purpose!

Something to keep in mind when one conducts menu engineering is that "the menu engineering process is never finished. Ingredient pricing will vary, and customer demographics and choices will continue to change, but it's up to you to stay up-to-date on everything."[222] In other words,

---

220 Bradley Turnwald, Danielle Boles, and Alia Crum, "Association Between Indulgent Descriptions and Vegetable Consumption: Twisted Carrots and Dynamite Beets," *JAMA Internal Medicine* 177, no. 8 (August 2017).

221 Ibid.

222 Ryan Andrews, "Menu Engineering: How to Increase Profits by 20 percent (Step-by-Step Guide)," Eat, April 15, 2019.

restaurant owners cannot assume that the ways things are now will continue to be the way things are in the future, including price, menu options, interest, and more. Constantly conducting analysis on the menu with careful attention to numbers is necessary in curating a menu that works for a restaurant. It's a continuous process.

Are you still thinking about that imaginary rich, chocolate cake from earlier? I am. But crafting a successful menu is no piece of cake, especially with all the shifts in customer preferences like interest in international flavors and healthy foods.[223] Due to the dynamic nature of customer preferences, competitive menus are in turn constantly evolving and the subject of experimentation. To truly adapt, restaurants must strike a balance between establishing a menu that both reflects their brand and identity while also catering to the changing needs of customers.

---

223 "IFT18: Generation Z Set To Impact The Future Of Food And Drink Innovation," Mintel, Mintel Group Ltd, July 16, 2018.

CHAPTER 16

SEASONALITY

One of my favorite stops for a sweet icy treat is Bedford Farms Ice Cream in Massachusetts. I have fond memories of walking to the shop from my high school soccer games and track meets to celebrate with my teammates over a generous portion of ice cream (even a loss deserves some ice cream). The great thing about the ice cream shop is that it constantly rotates flavors and offers seasonal varieties. Red raspberry chip, mocha chip, cinnamon sugar, French vanilla—you name it, they have it. There's almost always a line, even during the winter. Not a lot of ice cream shops can say that. I always look forward to indulging in my personal fall favorite, pumpkin ice cream. I never knew pumpkin would taste good in ice cream until a scoop of Bedford Farms changed me for life. Seasonal menus like these help generate that sense of excitement and anticipation. Since each new season brings new menu items, there's always something novel to look forward to, besides the classic flavors. You'll definitely find me there in October, devouring that pumpkin ice cream.

As mentioned in the local sourcing chapter, the perk about sourcing ingredients from the community is that it allows restaurants to alter their menus flexibly, and thus seasonally. "Featuring seasonal vegetables lets chefs keep their menus fresh and inspired throughout the year (which is in itself another trend: Seasonal locally sourced menus)," linking together the seasonality of produce to menus themselves.[224]

With this in mind, restaurants can "draw ideas and inspiration from local farmers and their crops during [the restaurant's] growing season as well as the varieties and growing seasons of more distant regions," since it opens up new possibilities.[225] Keeping up with seasonal trends is profitable for business. Restaurants can gain 26 percent more orders with seasonal menus.[226] The main benefits of a seasonal menu are that it keeps menu items fresh for customers, helps control costs since certain seasons are more expensive than others, allows for a chance to market new offerings more often, and connects restaurants with the community.[227]

With shorter supply chains and less emphasis on produce surviving transportation, restaurants are free to experiment with different produce in season. This opens up options for creativity and mixing up menu items to keep it interesting. Chef Nate Whitley at the Modern Hotel in Idaho is passionate about sourcing locally to create enticing new menu items.[228]

---

224 Mark Cooper, "Food for Thought: Trends in Menu Design," IIAC, January 16, 2018.

225 "Principles of Healthy, Sustainable Menus," Menus of Change, The Culinary Institute of America, accessed June 1, 2020.

226 Kristen Costa, "Why Your Restaurant Should Embrace Seasonal Menus," Upserve, Upserve, Inc., February 9, 2018.

227 Ibid.

228 "Sourcing Food Locally," Homegrown Stories, accessed June 1, 2020.

A benefit to sourcing locally is the diversity in wild products and the change in his menu from season to season. Customers are always getting fresh flavors of the season.

Whitley's "personal wild, seasonal favorites are trout and mushrooms. He includes those options on his menu whenever he can," since the nature of the menu is dynamic.[229] Whitley himself said that "the wild mushrooms in the summer, especially the morels here, are unique and every season a little different," highlighting the idea of celebrating different ingredients in different seasons.[230] And it's also celebrating the work of the local community and farmers. Whitley shared that "when you buy from local producers, you know you're buying something that was produced by a person that cares as much about what they're doing as you do."[231]

Keeping the menu interesting goes hand in hand with the marketing aspect. Hannah Spencer, a foodservice analyst at Mintel, shared that "seasonal menu items continue to be a key opportunity for operators to appeal to diners' interest in trying something new," attracting customers.[232] In addition, "operators should market seasonal items on menus and social media to encourage trial and purchasing by cross-generational diners," Spencer suggested. Restaurants can generate interest with "limited-time offers" and "seasonal" descriptors in their campaigns, adding a degree of urgency and exclusivity to try

---

229 Ibid.

230 Ibid.

231 Ibid.

232 "Seasonal Dining Trends - US - June 2019," Mintel, Mintel Group Ltd, July 16, 2018.

the newest item.[233] It switches the menu up and makes for great marketing material to push out when the season starts and let UGC (if photo– or review-worthy) take over the rest of the season to prompt other potential customers to "get them before they're gone!"

When I went apple picking with my family one autumn day (an original family outing, I know), a small restaurant nearby sourced those very apples for its seasonal menu. It propped up a large sign that read *Apple Cider Doughnuts Here!* Intrigued, we went inside. The restaurant had an open kitchen, so we could see each person preparing the different parts of the recipe transparently: creating the cider from the farmed apples, making the dough, frying. Sold. By the time they delicately packaged a couple of doughnuts into a brown paper bag, I couldn't wait to try one. And boy, was it good. Eating the doughnut was heaven. Incredibly soft to the touch, hot since it was freshly made, coated with cinnamon sugar that stuck to my fingers, and apple cider in every single bite—hands down the best doughnut I've ever had in my life. Even better since I knew the apples were freshly plucked the same day! Pushing out menu items like these during fall months was huge for the restaurant. The line was incredibly long due to so much demand from the apple pickers nearby. A seasonal item that got us through the door: the restaurant deserves apple-ause.

When it comes to cost, it's cheaper for restaurants to harvest produce when at the peak of its season (supply and demand), so following seasonal produce guides are helpful in cutting down expenses and maximizing the fruits and vegetables

---

233 Ibid.

at their best. It's also helpful to be familiar with produce that are in season year-round, including apples, lemons, and bananas.[234] This is useful to keep in mind if restaurants decide to keep certain core dishes the same and change others seasonally or combine different ingredients together.

By implementing a locally sourced seasonal menu, restaurants are able to foster deeper relationships with the community, an important initiative to support farmers and local businesses. Since restaurants can stir up interest and profit off seasonal menus in returns, the concept of creating shared valued appears again—uplifting stakeholders involved is embedded in business operations.

---

234 "What's in Season All Year Round [Seasonal Produce Guide]," Nature's Path, Nature's Path Foods, September 29, 2016.

EXPERIENTIAL DINING

CHAPTER 17

SERVICE/INTERACTION

———

I remember traveling to Maine with my family and stopping by a lobster roll shack. I absolutely love a good lobster roll, so I was extremely excited to get a bite of the New England specialty. Sounds great! But not too great when the server takes your order, forgets to tell the chef the menu items, puts the blame on you, and ignores your table when you need help. So even if the lobster roll tasted delicious, the customer experience is what I remember most vividly, almost a decade later after sitting at the outdoor wooden table covered with classic red and white checkered tablecloth.

To quote Maya Angelou, American poet, autobiographer, and civil rights activist, "I've learned that people will forget what you said, people will forget what you did, but people will never forget how you made them feel." Needless to say, it wasn't surprising to find the shack's Yelp page home to a range of negative and unimpressed reviews. This is one reason why I make it a practice to check for service in reviews today, since those interactions really do affect your overall experience. Next time I want a lobster roll in Maine, I'm rolling elsewhere.

Just because there's an increase in technology in the restaurant space, don't think human interaction is going away anytime soon. Service still matters and plays a role in a customer's relationship to a restaurant. Service falls under experiential dining because how customers, chefs, and staff interact with one another can go great lengths in defining one's perception of a restaurant.

But what does "service" entail? Accommodations, conversations, support, cleanliness, reliability, a sense of trust, and more are all part of service. Maximizing on service is important to cultivating a more personal experience for the customer. It's important to note that offering subpar service has greater impact today as well. It's not only that the customer will not likely return; they will make sure other people know about their lackluster experience as well. After all, customers can easily channel their opinions to social media and affect the restaurant's online presence with negative reviews.

* * *

Service can take many forms, including a community connection. Think about all-American diners that have been around for decades. While they might offer great hash browns and make your eggs just the way you like them, what sits at the heart of these restaurants is a connection with the community—that local charm and human touch that turns a simple meal into a personal experience.

For instance, Wally's Place, a bagel shop, has a special place South Hero, Vermont. It was named after owner Matt Bartle's grandfather, Walter "Wally" Niebling, who was well-known in the community for his generosity and support in donation initiatives.[235] Since its opening in 2008, the shop has been known for both its delicious offerings and a friendly service that lives up to the nature of Wally himself. These types of connections plant the seed in solidifying one's restaurant in the community: revolving around people first. This turns one-time customers into loyal customers for years.

* * *

Besides links with the community, service can take the form of an interactive experience. "Diners seem to be trending more and more toward interaction with restaurants and kitchens. I foresee more open kitchens, counters, and service led by back-of-house teams. This would include things like smaller tasting menus and more crafted experiences," asserted award-winning chef Dave Beran, owner of Dialogue and Pasjoli in Santa Monica, California.[236] Interaction between chefs and customers allows for more transparency and also individual experiences that help make restaurants stand out. Traditionally, chefs and customers are entirely separated with servers and staff being the middlemen in food delivery. Now with the emphasis on interaction-based service, everyone in the restaurant is involved in the dining experience; it's not only about the food itself.

I spoke with Andrea DeSimone, co-owner of Spinnaker, an upscale Mediterranean restaurant and inn located in Cape

---

235 "Home," Wally's Place Bagel & Deli, accessed June 1, 2020.

236 Regan Stephens, "These Will Be the Biggest Food Trends of 2020, According to Chefs," Food & Wine, Meredith Corporation, December 11, 2019.

Cod, Massachusetts. She's also a retail and restaurant broker, intersecting her interests of hospitality, real estate, and business. The special thing about DeSimone is that she is an incredibly warm, observant, and kind person. When I finished interviewing her, why she excels at what she does was clear. Without having ever met me, she made me feel like I knew her for years.

When I asked DeSimone about her views on service and connecting with customers in Spinnaker, she responded with a rhetorical question: "Why bother doing it if you're not going to have a personal connection with someone?" She extended this philosophy for not only the restaurant industry, but "any industry" and "any job." Value comes from building relationships. DeSimone added that it "makes life much more enjoyable," too. It was interesting to talk to DeSimone about this, since her answer actually overlaps with my own views. No matter what a person pursues, being able to connect with others in a meaningful way is critical, professionally and personally.

DeSimone shared with me that she writes a handwritten note thanking guests, delivered when the bill is presented. That magic of a personal note makes an incredible impression. "It's just another opportunity to talk to someone," DeSimone explained cheerfully. Of course, the dynamic depends on the service structure of a restaurant. DeSimone noted that it's more common to see this sort of attention to the customer experience in fine-dining, sit-down locations like Spinnaker versus in fast-casual or fast-food establishments.

She shared a story of a time she wrote a note for a guest. Turns out, the guest was a handwriting analyst and owned an art gallery down the street! The note itself sparked that conversation, showing the power of a thoughtful message. "We got to know each other," DeSimone said, something otherwise not possible by reaching out in building new relationships. Breaking down the supposed wall between owner and customer, DeSimone finds great satisfaction in connecting with others—not as mere guests but also as unique individuals with stories to share and lives to enrich. Spinnaker reminds us what it's like to be human, on a very moving level.

To DeSimone, it's only natural. "My mother taught me to write thank you notes," she explained. "So to me, that's how we present the bill before they swipe on the iPad." Therefore, while DeSimone does use technology in Spinnaker, she doesn't let it take away the importance of human interaction. She contends that while technology "can help in many situations," she doesn't "want to complicate it."

If anything, she's able to use technology to better her service. With a POS system in place, she was able to retrieve data on Spinnaker's "number one customer," since the system tracks all sorts of analytics and patterns. She and her team at Spinnaker celebrated the customer's hundredth visit with flowers and a thank you balloon, completely surprising the loyal guest. The usual customer does not track every single restaurant visit in a detailed spreadsheet (or maybe some do, who knows), so that special acknowledgement as a frequent diner can be an unexpected and pleasant surprise. "I did use the technology a little bit in that regard to better enhance the customer connection," DeSimone highlighted. She found a creative way to use the technology in line with her business's vision.

My main takeaway from DeSimone boiled down to this sentence: "Touch points matter to everyone in life, in general, to connect with people." Taking it outside of the scope of the restaurant industry, and even business in general, bonding with others in an essential part of life. Whether it be with a close friend or with a stranger met on public transportation, there's always room to learn, grow, and care.

Good service is essential to any business, a core part that finds value in human interaction. Ensuring quality service with proper staff training, more transparency, and more individualized experiences will help restaurants avoid impersonal, unmemorable interactions. After all, the 2017 Customer Service Barometer found that seven out of ten customers are more willing to spend money on companies that deliver great service, highlighting impacts on revenue.[237] So if restaurants want the dough, avoid cookie-cutter customer service at all costs.

---

237 "U.S. Consumers – Especially Millennials – Say Businesses Are Meeting Or Exceeding Their Service Expectations," American Express, American Express Company, December 15, 2017.

CHAPTER 18

WAIT TIME

———

At the end of my freshman year of college, I wanted to celebrate the end of finals with a good meal with friends. So I researched the best restaurants in the area, did my due diligence of evaluating reviews on Yelp, and made an executive decision for the collective: a small, yet highly reviewed Japanese restaurant not too far away. Perfect. Upon approaching the restaurant, we were shocked to find a line with at least fifteen people stretching outside the location. Looks like other people had the same idea. Unfortunately, there wasn't an option to reserve a table ahead of time, so the only option would be to wait—a wait that would be approximately forty to sixty minutes. Nope. My friends and I turned on our heels and entered a neighboring restaurant and were seated within five minutes. By the time we would have been seated at the Japanese restaurant, we were already enjoying our garlic naan and chicken curry with its competitor. A change of plans after all that research but a necessary action to avoid wasting time just waiting.

Today, customers still experience long wait times. While that may sound good at first, since getting people through the door is a challenge, it can be detrimental if the customer grows impatient and loses interest in the restaurant. An important distinction is actual wait time versus perceived wait time.

Perceived wait time relates to how long the customer believes to have waited, very variable from one person to the next.

> "According to Maister (1985), perceived waiting time depends on many factors such as whether the customer is occupied or not, waiting stage, whether the customer is anxious or not, whether the wait is certain or not, whether reason for the wait is explained or not, whether the customer is alone or not and finally the value of the service."[238]

Actual wait time, in contrast, is how long the customer waited in reality. Because of the subjective nature of perceived wait time, even if the wait time could be short in actuality, it could still be viewed longer. And if not deemed "acceptable" by the customer, wait time can lead to a decrease in customer satisfaction.[239] That's what restaurants are cautious of.

One way that restaurants combat long wait times is by employing automation in their operations: kiosks, iPad, and mobile ordering in the physical location, as discussed in the automation chapter. Doing so reduces wait time while also giving customers the time to make decisions comfortably.

---

238 T.M.B., Palawatta, "Waiting Times and Defining Customer Satisfaction," *Vidyodaya Journal of Management* 1, no. 1 (June 2015).

239 Ibid.

Spoken Cafe in Chicago, Illinois uses Toast's POS technology to help servers and employees during the cafe's busiest times. Owner Will Goodwin explained how: "Toast has made a huge impact on helping us move through the rush faster. We use handheld tablets to jump through the line and take orders before people get to the counter."[240] So while Spoken Cafe does bring in an abundance of customers, it uses POS technology to avoid customers waiting in line and keeping it moving. Goodwin noted that "the average ticket time during our rush is about 8.5 minutes, which is much better than it was with our pen-and-paper system, although I wasn't able to actually measure it back then," since Spoken Cafe now uses Toast's kitchen display screens to communicate customer orders fast.[241] Investing in time-saving technology makes an incredible difference.

Depending on the style and demand for a restaurant, reservation systems like OpenTable, Resy, and Eat are options for integrating technology and managing an influx of diners to best manage customer flow.[242] Reservation systems are helpful in seating large parties easily while also accommodating for walk-ins and staying organized. It's also great in analyzing trends in seating to figure out how to best allocate staff and necessary supplies based on performance.[243] Training staff to seat customers efficiently can also solve this issue, and so can having proper signage regarding reservations, walk-ins, and takeout options.

---

240 "Spoken Cafe Busts the Morning Rush with Toast," Toast, Toast, Inc., accessed June 1, 2020.

241 Ibid.

242 Colleen Egan, "How to Reduce Wait Time at Your Restaurant," Square, Square Inc., accessed June 1, 2020.

243 Ibid.

Andrea Johnston, the chief operating officer at OpenTable, announced that in 2019, the company reached a "major milestone" of "10 billion diners seated, using our software. To put that in perspective, that's more than the world's population."[244] She added that "this year alone, we sat over 283 million diners who gave more than 13 million reviews. This uncovered a treasure trove of food trends and shifts in behavior to provide insightful context as to how people are eating in 2019."[245] Her words underscore how much more prevalent tools like reservation systems are being used in the restaurant space and also how analytics can be used to find new trends in food.

To aid customer decision-making, Google introduced a feature in 2017 that shows a restaurant's most popular times. It works by tracking where users are with phones (Android or iOS) using Google apps and then using "that data to show users' relevant information and [stitching] it together to work out whether there is traffic."[246] I use this feature all the time when deciding where to eat. It's helpful to know that information in advance for customers to plan out their dining experience in light of busiest restaurant times.

Wait times are not an issue that all restaurants face, but knowing how customer behavior is affected by it is important. Because even if a restaurant employs great social media marketing and has a flawless reputation online, a customer is willing to wait for only so long.

244 Lisa Singh, "What's On Your Plate? OpenTable Reveals Dining Trends for 2019," OpenTable, OpenTable Inc., December 2, 2019.

245 Ibid.

246 Andrew Griffin, "Google Popular Times: New Maps Tool Gathers Location Data To Help People Beat Queues," *Independent*, July 30, 2015.

Wait times, however, can be used expertly to generate interest and reinforce the idea that sometimes waiting for something worthwhile makes it all the better, like at Yume Wo Katare, the ramen noodle shop mentioned at the beginning of the book. Chef Tsuyoshi Nishioka at Yume Wo Katare believes that waiting is part of the experience, stirring up anticipation for a delectable meal, so its lines often stretch out the door thanks to its unique eating experience.[247] It works in Yume Wo Katare's case since diners confess to waiting hours to get a chance at experiencing the magic of the ramen institution, often satisfied after the long-awaited meal. But other times, waiting can just drive customers out the door if the customer does not find it justifiable. Ultimately, wait time carries weight in the overall customer experience.

---

247 Andrea Shea, "Can Finishing A Big Bowl Of Ramen Make Dreams Come True?" *National Public Radio*, July 25, 2014.

CHAPTER 19

DESIGN

Flatbread Company is a pizza chain that places great emphasis on organic, high-quality ingredients and local sourcing when possible. Its location in Bedford, Massachusetts is one I frequented with my family, since the menu items were consistently delectable. My favorite part about Flatbread Co. is just the ambiance itself—warm colors, wooden chairs and tables, soft lighting. We always ask to be seated near the hand-built clay oven, a centerpiece that engulfs the attention of the room, for good reason. That's where the action is: dough tossed, toppings placed, and pizza cooked in the massive oven. Feeling the warmth from the fire as you watch your pizza being made right in front of you is incredibly satisfying. Just by design itself, from the wooden furniture to opening up the pizza-making process (complete with clay oven) near the seating area, made such a difference in the experience and also reflects what kind of restaurant Flatbread Co. is: natural, comforting, and transparent—reflective of its branding and mission while also incorporating interesting elements that other pizza places in the area did not. Innovative while also staying true to brand, Flatbread Co. strikes the perfect balance of maintaining identity while adapting.

"In general, the restaurants that are the most agile in responding to design trends have performed the best in a tough economic period," according to Gourmet Marketing, highlighting the importance of adapting, or at least responding in a way that is consistent with the branding and messaging of the business.[248] Key questions restaurants should ask before implementing design trends include, "What do you want customers to walk away with?" "How will design affect restaurant perception?" and "Does it stay true to the message you are trying to convey?" Thinking about these questions will help owners and restaurant leadership sell the image that best captures the essence of the business. This image needs to be consistent in both a physical location and social media space to stay competitive, memorable, and true to the brand. So when it comes to design of a restaurant, it's not about buying the most modern-looking light fixtures or carefully positioning empty mason jars on a windowsill to "be with the times." Instead of focusing on individual parts, communicating the overall branding in a cohesive way helps customers gain insight into the restaurant's identity.

"Restaurant design is an important part of marketing strategies and efforts to attract and retain customers" when times are challenging, Gourmet Marketing asserted.[249] Doing so separates restaurants from competition. And it doesn't have to be expensive. One trend is toward fabric and ceiling covers that can be replaced easily and with little cost to offer new looks. The idea of a "transformable restaurant" is garnering

---

248 "Restaurant Design Trends," Restaurant Essentials, Gourmet Marketing, accessed June 1, 2020.

249 Ibid.

interest, which simply means being able to convert a space for different occasions, from parties to culinary classes hosted in the space. Investing in easily replaceable coverings saves time and money in exchange for a new and intriguing atmosphere. But at the same time, restaurants should be wary of switching up their design too much, especially if already solidifying a certain brand successfully. Key features that feed into the restaurant brand should remain constant, including the color scheme, certain symbols or images, or general atmosphere.

The best way to think about this is in terms of defining a target market, as Maciej Godlewski had discussed in the "Digital Strategy" chapter, applicable not just to social media and outreach but also to business direction overall. How that market may respond to the design of a restaurant helps narrow down what image would attract and keep such customers. After all, "to enhance customer experience in meaningful ways, it's important for restaurant operators to have an accurate picture of who their diners are, what they want and how their brand's ethos stands out from competitors," a Restaurant Dive article stressed.[250]

For example, say you're a cafe on a college campus. Having access to charging outlets, a welcoming and social atmosphere, and investing in appropriate lighting would be a helpful way to solidify the shop as a go-to working spot for college students, simply by what it offers besides the dining experience. On the other hand, if your restaurant is focused on providing new twists on classic French dishes that targets

---

250 Emma Liem Beckett, "6 restaurant trends that could turn tables in 2019," Restaurant Dive, Industry Dive, January 7, 2019.

young adults, combining both vintage and modern elements together will help sell that concept and intrigue that market. Creative ideas are endless but can be more targeted with an audience in mind. "Design" of a restaurant can include lighting, chairs, tables, flooring, walls, decor, colors, the layout itself and more. All these factor into creating a certain ambience and atmosphere.

Other design trends include overlapping sustainability with visuals. Investing in reclaimed wood, an in-house garden, and recycled materials are some ways to go green and pique interest. Avenue Restaurant in Clayton, Missouri, for example, is one institution that embodies sustainability in a multitude of ways, beyond sourcing locally. From using energy- and water-saving equipment in the kitchen to sourcing locally and hyperlocally, Avenue Restaurant practices environmentally conscious practices across the board. In addition, "Almost all of their furniture has been given a second life through repair and repurposing, and their walls are graced with antique barn wood."[251] Avenue cares about their environmental impact, reducing their waste and their energy consumption whenever possible," as reflected in their design as well.[252]

"Instagrammable" features in restaurants are becoming more and more popular. What does this mean? Connecting to the chapter on social media marketing, Instagram is one platform on which restaurants can be discovered and shared with the world through UGC. Restaurants offering features that invite customers to take photos helps increase the likelihood of being

---

251 "Avenue Restaurant," Green Dining Alliance, accessed June 1, 2020.

252 Ibid.

shared on social media. This can be particularly impactful if a food or social media influencer is able to market the institutions to their audience and use hashtags for even more exposure.

Pietro NoLita, a fifties-style New York bar and eatery, for example, specializes in "Healthy Italian Cuisine." But that's not the attention-grabbing part. After all, New York boasts an abundance of Italian restaurants. So Pietro NoLita differentiates itself with a distinct theme: all pink. Everything in the restaurant is pink: the walls, benches, stools, flowers, napkins. Its social media and website pages stay consistent with bold pink as well, part of the carefree, fun, and bold branding that attracts people all over the world to take photos and experience a splash of pink in their lives.[253]

Pink is just one example of an Instagrammable feature, or in this case, a theme. It could be a design based on a certain era, eye-catching murals, neon signs, or other statement features that invite customers to create content to share with their followers on various social media platforms. Cultivating a photo-worthy restaurant goes great lengths in reeling in new customers, since social media's reach is so vast and impressionable. And sometimes the visuals of a restaurant get customers through the door, even before looking at or pondering about the actual food.

> "Mike Kelly, co-founder and CEO of State of Mind Partners, said that one way to remain true to the brand is by not paying influencers — Instagram users with thousands or even millions of followers

---

253 "Healthy Italian Cuisine," Pietro NoLita, accessed June 1, 2020.

> — to come to your restaurant. An authentic social
> media presence can also help restaurants expand
> into new markets by introducing the brand to new
> customers while adding special touches relevant
> to the community."[254]

By leveraging the power of social media in a genuine way, restaurants can reach new customers through a design that is interesting to a specific target market and on brand. One thing to keep in mind is that while "the trend is largely limited to small restaurants," chains like Taco Bell are "trying to reach millennials who live in urban areas with its Cantinas, which often feature photogenic wall art," revealing how even bigger companies are taking note of what impactful, targeted designs can do for business.[255]

* * *

In a personal example, at the University of Illinois at Urbana-Champaign, there's a craft coffee shop on campus called BrewLab Coffee. For coffee enthusiasts, it's said to be very good. But let me be honest: I rarely drink coffee (let's check again in five years, though). So while a student there, I really had no inclination to go to BrewLab, let alone any coffee shop. Of course, it offered more than just coffee, but I could gain access to those other options in many other places (competition, remember). Plus, my freshman dorm was located on the other side of campus, so it would be quite the trek to make a special visit. I already lived across from the campus

---

254 Amelia Lucas, "Restaurants are investing in photogenic decor to attract Instagram users," *CNBC*, April 19, 2019.

255 Ibid.

gym at that time, so there was no need for an additional leg day. A lot of factors (or arguably just excuses) drove me to never enter BrewLab. However, there was an instance when I walked by the shop on the way back from visiting a friend.

Walking by, I looked inside the window (thankfully I didn't make awkward eye contact with anyone). I was immediately intrigued, since one glance into the shop offered so much to look at. As someone who loves exploring and analyzing nicely designed spaces, I decided to go in and check it out for a better view.

The friendly face of the barista greeted me as I walked in, to which I instantly responded with a smile of my own. Already warm. I then absorbed everything around me as I stood in line. It was small but did not feel cramped at all. The white walls and plentiful lights opened and brightened the space up. All sorts of small- to medium-sized succulents and potted plants were neatly arranged around the shop, lending them-selves to a very fresh and modern atmosphere. Some of them were even for sale. A black letter board mounted on the wall contrasted with white characters to communicate the simple menu easily. Customers could see how the baristas crafted each beverage since there were no divisive walls.

This design connects with the trend toward transparency and open-concept kitchens as "more and more, people want to see how the food is being made," asserted Allen Sherwin, Michigan State University professor of culinary manage-ment.[256] Customers "want to feel like they're a part of the

---

256 Darcy Schild, "10 food and restaurant trends that will define how people eat in 2020," Insider, Insider Inc., November 11, 2019.

experience, not just tucked away having their food magically brought to them."[257] It was open and helped facilitate conversation between baristas and customers, allowing for a personal connection.

On top of this, beverages were served in glass or white cups to keep up with its simple image. No bulky cash register here! The cashier used an iPad with a POS system to take orders, following the automation trend. Wooden tables added to the natural effect while modern chairs and stools added a cutting industrial aspect, reinforcing its sharp image. Students sat talking with friends, studying, and just enjoying their respective drinks, a social yet also productive place to be. Whiteboard walls all over the shop invited customers to express themselves to the world at their heart's content, whether it be in fun drawings or inspirational quotes. The wall, collecting thoughts and ideas throughout the day, promoted imagination and a sense of community. This exemplifies the trend toward memorable visuals, since a whiteboard wall is unique and also an interesting, ever-changing statement piece.

When it was finally my turn in line, my initial interest in design morphed into interest in the menu. Why not try something out? I opted for a chamomile tea and made small talk with the barista as they made it meticulously, poured it into their signature sturdy white cup, and handed it to me. I added a touch of honey, found a cozy spot, and felt a sense of contentment. Ultimately, a blend of both a natural warmth, contemporary freshness, and invitation for creativity is what my eyes concluded BrewLab to be, even before taking my first sip of the hot tea.

---

257 Ibid.

BrewLab's website shares that: "It is in our heart to create a space where… quality coffee is brewed, stories are shared, and our lives are enriched."[258] It's interesting how my initial reactions to its design matched closely to how the shop wanted to be perceived. Branding is incredibly important in that sense, since it offers so much insight into what the restaurant stands for—in BrewLab's case, a space to bring people together and deliver quality on many levels, from drink to forming connections. And it was easy to see that walking in.

I kept going back to BrewLab throughout the semester to work and hang out with friends, since I appreciated its calming ambiance and chamomile tea so much. Great menu options can bring in customers, but they're not the only way to attract them. Restaurants, coffee shops, cafes, and any food institution you can name needs to be competitive on multiple fronts, including on the design and branding end.

But that doesn't mean that restaurant design overshadows the quality of the menu, since design can only contribute so much to branding and customer perception. Going back to Elizabeth Tilton and Jessica Abell from the "Breakdown" chapter, making an impression on the customer starts right away as in "those first interactions, you have ten seconds to make an impact" to "tell the consumer why they should walk into your door." It does not only apply on social media but also in person.

Walking through the door after a single glance and buying a drink is a win on BrewLab's part. Returning throughout the

---

258 "Experience," Brew Lab Coffee, accessed June 1, 2020.

semester after a satisfying experience? Now that's a victory. After all, BrewLab's clean and inviting atmosphere is what first reeled me in. But its delicious chamomile tea on top of this warm ambiance is what kept me returning, finding the comfort to both enjoy the tea and study productively in such a space incredibly refreshing. And who knows, maybe next time I'll try the coffee.

Design has incredible impact on how a customer views and relates to any business, not just restaurants. In an age of technology, this is especially critical, whether it be in a photogenic atmosphere or conveying how the design reflects a restaurant's overall mission, like sustainability. Le Cordon Bleu explains that at the end of the day, "not only will the design of a restaurant affect how the venue is perceived" but it "can even influence how much customers are willing to order and pay for."[259] Design strategically!

---

259 "The secret psychology behind restaurant design," Le Cordon Bleu, Le Cordon Bleu International B.V., accessed June 1, 2020.

CHAPTER 20

UNIQUE SELLING PROPOSITION

Customers seek something new and unconventional that makes going to a restaurant (versus online food delivery and cooking at home) worthwhile. Hudson Riehle, the senior vice president of research at the National Restaurant Association, asserted that customers go to restaurants for convenience and socialization.[260] Even with the trend of online delivery, "people do still crave being at a physical restaurant for being around other people, for that atmosphere you can't recreate at home, and for special occasions."[261] Riehle argued that with trends toward technology to facilitate food orders, the social aspect of restaurants is heightened as a result.

With this in mind, experience at a restaurant deserves more emphasis now than ever since it brings people together to

---

260 Darcy Schild, "10 food and restaurant trends that will define how people eat in 2020," Insider, Insider Inc., November 11, 2019.

261 Ibid.

share a moment. So what moment, adventure, or experience will the restaurant create for the customer to form those memories? What separates it from the competition? "Differentiating on experience can be a lot of different things. In some respects, it's that Instagrammable or Snapchatable moment… but in some cases, it can just be simply better service, better quality of execution in the restaurant," stated David Portalatin, vice president and food industry analyst at the NPD Group.[262] This chapter looks into ways restaurants can distinguish themselves, since the competition is no longer just other restaurants but online delivery as well.

Portalatin's words funnel into the idea of creating a unique selling proposition (USP), which is making an impression on customers by standing out. The foundational service structure of restaurants fall in cafe or self-serve, fast food, casual dining, fine dining, family style, the emerging fast-casual dining category, or some other blend of the former, to name a few.[263] The USP restaurants provide works off these service structures to present something innovative to the customer. In other words, it is not the service structure itself that offers the unique and differentiating factor, but rather how it is adapted to differentiate itself from competitors and add value to the customer. This can take the form of many aspects, including signature dishes, service, sustainability, price, recognition, tradition, convenience, and concept.[264]

---

262 Emma Liem Beckett, "6 restaurant trends that could turn tables in 2019," Restaurant Dive, Industry Dive, January 7, 2019.

263 "Topic 1: 5 Types of Service," Chefmanship Academy, Unilever Food Solutions, accessed June 1, 2020.

264 "Creating a Unique Selling Proposition For Your Restaurant," Grubhub for Restaurants, Grubhub Holdings Inc., January 3, 2019.

Restaurants are not single-noted institutions, so often the USP for a restaurant is a distinctive, unique blend of these factors. For instance, take an affordable, locally sourced vegan eatery (price and sustainability factors) or a diner that has been around for ages and established itself as the town's best spot for American comfort food (recognition and tradition factors). In other words, the blend of USP factors is special to and characteristic of the restaurant's branding, mission, and offerings itself. Let's explore each with current examples. Again, keep in mind that these factors are often at play with one another, whether it be in cause or effect, adding to its complexity and ability to stand out from the crowd.

SIGNATURE DISHES

Nothing gets people talking (or eating) like food, especially if the food is unique in its adaptation or signature to a restaurant. Mike's Pastry, a legendary spot in Boston, is a prime example. Go into Boston and you're likely to see people (preciously) holding a white box with blue lettering, tied firmly with a string: the bakery's distinct packaging. Founded in 1946, the Italian bakery is home to all sorts of baked treats, from almond macaroons to chocolate-dipped biscotti. But its signature sweet delight that brings in much attention is its famous cannoli.

Overall, cannoli connoisseurs and pastry enthusiasts satisfy their sweet tooth cravings here, as evidenced by the long lines of tourists and locals alike. My childhood memories living in Massachusetts take me back to the humble institution where my family and I would stop for a sweet treat before exploring Boston. So good!

What's important about signature dishes as part of a USP is that they are weaved into the overall branding of a restaurant, explained by Gourmet Marketing.[265] Mike's Pastry shares that "Michael Mercogliano (the 'Mike' behind the famed Mike's Pastry) created the one-of-a-kind cannoli that keeps loyal Bostonians and tourists coming from around the world to enjoy," the bakery's most prized item offered in eighteen flavors as of 2020.[266]

Successful signature dishes are important since they help up-sell other items, allow customers to associate the food itself with the restaurant over time, attract media attention, prompt UGC over social media, and encourage customers to spend more money on trying other items, knowing the signature item is bound to bring great satisfaction. Perfecting and staying consistent with its famous cannoli and other baked goods has allowed Mike's Pastry to expand to more locations since it *cannoli* take so much demand.

SERVICE

Don't underestimate the power of interaction and attention to detail, since they impact the customer experience. While Chick-fil-A is known for its food despite its criticism, it prides itself in customer service, a driving factor for its success. As of 2019, Chick-fil-A ranks number one in the American Customer Satisfaction Index's survey for four years in a row.[267]

---

265 Matthew, "The Promotional Power of a Signature Dish," Gourmet Marketing, August 30, 2013.

266 "History," Mike's Pastry, accessed June 1, 2020.

267 Kate Taylor, "Chick-fil-A is taking over America by offering the best customer service in fast food," Business Insider, Insider Inc., June 26, 2019.

Mark Kalinowski, founder of Kalinowski Equity Research, explained that "little things like being told 'please' and 'thank you' — it feels like you're appreciated as a customer and a human being at Chick-fil-A."[268]

Chick-fil-A has standards when it comes to service, allowing customers in all its locations to experience the same quality of care and attention and building a reputation across the board. And customers notice this. Kalinowski stresses that "especially in today's very complex world, it's just very nice to be able to go to a place where you feel appreciated."[269] Even though it seems basic, training employees and restaurant management in fostering a positive connection with the customer opens the door for leaving a personal impact. After all, customers want to be respected and have their needs met during their dining experience. While service may not be the primary motivation in customer decision-making, it does contribute to the customers' overall satisfaction and likelihood of returning and forming loyal customers.

A personal example of excellent service (and food!) is a small, unassuming Japanese restaurant called Sushi House, located in Rockville, Maryland. I highly recommend the Barcelona Roll for those who love heat: spicy tuna, eel, pickled ginger, and avocado, topped with a slice of jalapeño to set fire to the taste buds. Each roll is freshly crafted with care, expertise, and passion, tasted in every single bite. To top the experience and connect with the USP of service, the server was very friendly and attentive, mentioning that she has been working there for

---

268 Ibid.

269 Ibid.

over ten years. She even remembered my family's orders from the last time we visited, two months prior! Quality service, clean atmosphere, and mouth-watering options make Sushi House competitive and literally on a roll.

SUSTAINABILITY

The core question in relation to USP: what actions is the restaurant taking on the sustainability front to make it stand out? Dig Inn, a chain of sustainable restaurants founded by Adam Eskin, is a great example.[270] Dig Inn cultivates relationships with all its one hundred-plus farmers, buying produce locally (three hundred-mile radius from each respective restaurant). Since Dig Inn sources locally, it has the benefit of being able to change its menu more often according to the season's harvest, as discussed in the "Seasonality" chapter, keeping options interesting and using produce when it's at its best.

Sustainability is at the center of this restaurant's branding and operations, something that separates it as a green leader. Furthermore, Dig Inn is clear about this mission on its website, stating that its ultimate goal is "to change the food system by investing in waste reduction; a sustainable future of farming; and a locally-sourced, vegetable-driven menu."[271] With this branding, customers discover that dining at Dig Inn is more than a good meal: it's fresh (served within forty-eight hours of harvest, seasonal), it's personal (local community connection, farmer relationship), it's health conscious (supports organic practices, transparent), and it's green (smaller supply chain, limited waste). What's not to love?

----

270 "We're Making A Difference," Dig, accessed June 1, 2020.

271 Ibid.

PRICE

While it's easy to think that low prices mean less money reeled in, they can actually have the opposite effect if more customers are interested simply because of the possibility of saving more. Take Falafel Inc, based in Washington, DC. Its menu is simple, yet grabbing: nothing is over $4. Customers can buy a falafel bowl for a whopping $4, a sandwich for $3, and specialty zaatar fries and other sides for $3.[272] This makes it a go-to cheap eats spot in such a busy city like DC. What's even better about Falafel Inc is that a portion of each purchase is donated to refugees around the world. The chain brands itself as the "world's first falafel fast-casual food social enterprise" partnered with the World Food Programme to aid in this pressing issue.[273]

However, the competitive pricing and donations for the cause makes one wonder if it's able to profit. After all, there is a line between offering cheap prices and being able to break even. Founder Ahmad Akshar shared that he "can keep prices low by running an efficient operation with fewer hours" and by "relying on economies of scale to get the most bang for his and his customers' buck," explained Becky Krystal from the *Washington Post*.[274] "Falafel Inc. routinely makes about 3,000 falafel balls daily (six on a sandwich, eight in a bowl), though that can increase by several thousand on busy days."[275] And that was in 2017. Since then, demand has grown after more

---

272 "Fresh Ingredients. Authentic food. Real impact," Falafel Inc., accessed June 1, 2020.

273 Ibid.

274 Becky Krystal, "This $3 falafel sandwich is one of the best cheap meals in Washington," the *Washington Post*, June 16, 2017.

275 Ibid.

customers fala-fell in love with its tasty offerings, affordable prices, and cause to help refugees worldwide, and Falafel Inc expanded to more locations.

RECOGNITION

Boasting local, regional, or national acclaim is another motivator for customers to visit. Founded in 1925, Frank Pepe Pizzeria Napoletana from New Haven, Connecticut, is not just any pizza place—it's a national treasure. Frank Pepe Pizzeria Napoletana is regarded as the nation's best pizzeria by the Daily Meal and is known for its signature white clam pizza.[276] Since then, it has garnered more publicity and praise to expand to other areas on the East Coast.

After seeing it featured on television, I actually visited the original New Haven location with my family while passing through Connecticut. While I enjoy a decent pizza like the next person, I normally would not go out of my way for it. However, because I was hearing such great reviews, I just had to check it out and see what the fuss was about. That was the first time I have ever tried white clam pizza, and it was a satisfying meal indeed. The fact that I made a special stop to see what the hype was about in the first place exemplifies how recognition, awards, and positive acclaim drive customer behavior. It serves as proof that if so many other customers had a great experience, I most likely would as well, and the confidence in this is a driving motivator. Frank Pepe benefits from the great recognition

---

276 Arthur Bovino and Dan Myers, "The 101 Best Pizzas in America," The Daily Meal, Tribune Publishing, September 27, 2019.

earned through the original differentiating factor of delicious, New Haven-style pizzas.

TRADITION

Tradition has different definitions. One relates to restaurants establishing themselves over time as a generational or family-owned restaurant. The other is staying true to authentic flavors and cuisine from a part of the world. Kabob n Karahi, an unassuming halal Pakistani-Indian restaurant in Silver Spring, Maryland exemplifies both spheres of tradition. The family restaurant stays true to its Pakistani-Indian roots, offering a variety of spicy curries, tender kabobs, and flavorful karahi (traditional stew) served in generous portions.

While living in Maryland, I loved stopping by Kabob n Karahi with my family, never growing tired of its options. My family would share multiple dishes so we each could try the different yet equally tantalizing menu items. Whether it be Lahori choley (chickpeas) paired with naan or well-spiced chicken karahi, one thing is for certain: quality is consistent across the board. My personal favorite menu item is the incredibly juicy lamb chops, marinated and grilled to perfection—undeniably (and without exaggeration) the best lamb chops my taste buds have had the honor of tasting (second to my mom's impeccable lamb chops, of course).

The rich blend of spices connects customers with Indian and Pakistani cuisine both in heart and in stomach, something that generates the loyalty for customers to go there for years. If you ever find yourself in that area, give Kabob n Karahi a visit. Don't be fooled by its casual and unassuming atmosphere. The restaurant is a hidden gem bursting with quality food that other Indian and Pakistani restaurants in the area simply cannot match.

CONVENIENCE

Convenience can take many forms, including grab-and-go items for busy individuals or turning to automation for increased efficiency (online ordering, kiosks, etc.). Paradita Eatery, a fast-casual Peruvian hotspot in Emeryville, California, exemplifies this. Chef and owner Carlos Altamirano, responsible for multiple highly recognized restaurants in the Bay Area, knows there is a desire and a need to provide convenient options to customers in the area.[277] Therefore, Paradita offers three main features that make sure that customers can gain easy access to their foods no matter their schedule or where they are: grab-and-go items, prepaid pickup, and online ordering.

First, they offer numerous to-go and catered items. Altamirano emphasized that the restaurant works to ensure that flavor is not compromised with the increased convenience associated with this option, as "Paradita has to provide meals that maintain their integrity over time."[278] Customers can buy their to-go options knowing they will stay fresh and just as tasty when consumed outside the restaurant.

The Peruvian restaurant takes convenience a step further by offering prepaid pickup that allows customers to select meal

---

277 "About Us," Paradita Eatery, accessed June 1, 2020.

278 Devon Flaherty, "How Far Can the Grab-and-Go Trend Go?" QSR, Journalistic, Inc., November 2018.

items beforehand to pick up at the restaurant from a more extensive menu than its grab-and-go selection. This gives customers more choice, adding in an online element.

Third, Paradita takes advantage of online ordering by Grubhub and Caviar to widen its access to customers and (literally) deliver delicious Peruvian food. By using these three features expertly, Paradita maximizes on providing both delicious food and convenience to its customers, distinguishing itself from less-accommodating competitors in the area.

CONCEPT

When discussing the concept of a restaurant, multiple factors are involved: theme, aesthetic, experience, ambience, style, food, and more. Combining different aspects in a unique way can be a concept itself, like a fast-casual Turkish cuisine, an ice cream shop that locally sources, or modernizing classic Korean dishes in a fine-dining setting. The options to explore creative combinations are endless! And quite fun as well. Besides these combinations, concept can also be a restaurant revolving around a single element, including product, color, or time period. It is a concept so long as the focal point ties the overall experience together cohesively, not just in one aspect. If not, it is simply a theme.

One example of a concept (revolving around a single food) is S'MAC (Sarita's Macaroni & Cheese) in New York. Opened in 2006, S'MAC serves different varieties of one of America's favorite staples: macaroni and cheese. All-American, 4 Cheese, Mediterranean, Masala, Buffalo Chicken—S'MAC offer all sorts of options in varying sizes for customers to order via kiosk, pick-up, or online delivery.[279] There's even a Build Your Own option, granting customers the reins to construct their ideal bowl of mac and cheese. S'MAC accommodates dietary restrictions (vegan, dairy, gluten), so each customer will be sure to find a mac perfect for satisfying their cravings. As if it couldn't get any better, the warm, gooey, cheesy delight is served in a sizzling cast iron skillet. Just thinking of what that would sound and look like makes me want to buy a plane ticket to New York right now. Wow.

In S'MAC, the furniture consists of wooden tables and bright accent chairs, with pops of orange and yellow in accent decor throughout the modern yet casual space. All elements together bring a sense of comfort and nostalgia many associate with mac and cheese. The success of the concept in its execution allows the eatery to continue pulling in customers for over a decade. After all, when was the last time you've eaten at a place that serves exclusively macaroni and cheese? Exactly. This differentiating factor invites mac and cheese lovers from all over to devote undivided attention to a classic that has been a side dish for too long. And people are hungry for it.

These are just few notable ways of differentiation that are visible to customers and effectively used. These factors are often intermingled to truly provide a unique experience to the customer. Next time you find yourself at a restaurant, take a minute to examine what brought you there in the first place. When you leave, assess if you would return and why. It's interesting how simple, reflective questions from the customer perspective can actually inform restaurant decisions, including cultivating an effective USP.

---

279 "Our Story," S'MAC, accessed June 1, 2020.

FINAL WORDS

For the carnivores out there, a steak dinner is incomplete without proper accompaniments, preferences dependent on the person. Garlic potatoes? A classic sauce? Pasta? Vegetables? Each component serves a different purpose but complements the others in its own way. Similarly, the trends outlined in the book may appear separated at the surface. Looking deeper, you'll find that many are actually very much interconnected with each other. As more overlap, more flavors of current trends develop.

Within the five broad trend categories featured, there was so much to unpack. You're able to close this book with greater insights into various trends, relevant examples, restaurants to check out, and perhaps some quality puns along the way. But it's not over. In fact, there is so much more to discover, within the customer context and beyond.

The restaurant industry is a constantly evolving segment of both the economy and culture. Whether it be in rapidly changing technologies, or adapting to marketing techniques to boost interest and sales, restaurants are more than just a menu and a kitchen. The customers are at the center of what defines a restaurant: actions, preferences, and more. Restaurants are constantly seeking to solidify themselves in a bustling industry. It is the customer who has the power to redefine a business. How these restaurants adapt to these forces determines their ability to succeed. The clock is ticking.

* * *

Sudden, entirely new shifts in the environment and customer can be especially detrimental, as during the COVID-19 pandemic. Restaurants were faced with a completely new set of forces to adapt to rapidly. The lack of in-person traffic, social distancing, safety guidelines in effect, falling supply chains, and more pushed businesses to the edge. A number of trends we've discussed played significant roles during this time:

- Surge in online ordering and takeout options

- Emboldened digital strategy, website, and social media presence

- Heightened community support online and in person

- Need to monitor inventory and data trends with technology

- Savings from limited, in-demand menu offerings

- Questioning what a "new normal" means for the industry

Restaurant tools and practices are a reflection of customer wants and needs in many ways. As Henry David Thoreau once wrote, "things do not change; we change." The root of change is human. The customer has the power to drive significant change over time. Price, convenience, offerings, preferences, impact, differential factors, meaningful connections, online presence—what will we determine to be essential as a population?

The *steaks* are raised, competition sizzling. It's now up to restaurants to adapt and make the cut.

BOOK ACKNOWLEDGMENTS

Setting sail on the journey of writing your first nonfiction book, you quickly learn what keeps the boat afloat: the people. I'm thankful for all the support I've received to make publishing *Restaurant Redefined* a reality.

First, a heartfelt thanks to my parents, Syed Jalal and Asma, for their unconditional support and enthusiasm in all my endeavors. You inspire me to shoot for the stars and never stop learning. Thank you to my brothers, Haroon and Faraaz, for constantly cheering me on and radiating positivity.

A sincere thanks to my fellow brothers at Phi Gamma Nu, the professional business fraternity that helped me grow in astounding ways and make incredible friendships.

Thank you to my wonderful interviewees who shared their valuable time and insights to enrich and bring the book to life.

I would like to express deep gratitude to Eric Koester. Thank you for mentoring me on how to produce a work with both passion and impact. I'm so grateful for all the help from New Degree Press, especially Cassandra Casswell and Linda Berardelli.

And thank you to the family, friends, mentors, and everyone who made publishing this book possible. This could not have been accomplished without you.

Agastya Brahmamdam
Ahsen Kocaman
Aidan Lawrence
Alexa Sorokwasz
Alexis Johnson
Aliyah Mohiuddin
Allen Li
Amna Khawaja & Family
Amogh Dendukuri
Ana Ugarte
Andrea DeSimone
Andrew Betbadal
Andrew Goodwin
Angelica Saggers
Anirvin Sikha
Anisa Choksi
Anisha Sullivan
Ankeeta Lal
Anna Riedl
Anna Tran
Annanta Budhathoki
Aroosha Rana & Family

Asma Bukhari
Ata Chowdhry
Atiqur Javaid & Family
Avery Schoenherr
Ayse Ecer
Ayusha Ayalur
Bao Anh Ho
Bilal Khan
Billy O'Donnell
Brandon Seuring
Brandon Shumate
Caleb DeRuiter
Cassidee M. Grunwald
Charles Lally
Christine Zhu
Colin Fischer
Cristopher Herrera
Daniel S. Hess
David Dalmaso
David Hussey
Elizabeth Tilton
Emi McSwain

Eric Koester
Faraaz Bukhari
Fatima Khan
Fatima Sultana & Moham-
med Qameruddin
Gina Miklasz
Hamzah Raza
Hannah McCurdy
Hannah Wolfe
Haroon Bukhari
Ibrahim Farooq Mohsin
Italia Kozarski
Ivana Wijedasa
J. Elizabeth Mascoli
Jason Lim
Jessica Abell
Jinghong He
Joely Centracchio
John Gehman
John Lampros
Jonah Fialkow
Justin Huang
Justyna Borowski
Kasturi Thonangi
Kayla Gonzalez
Keri Vornadore
Lam Tran
Lana Xing
Lancelot Daley
M. H. Khalil & Family
Maciej Godlewski
Maddie Garvey

Madeleine Sanderson
Malakut Khizar
Mansoor Kirmani & Family
Mary Dant
Matthew Mercure
Matthew Uthupan
Max O'Hern
Maya Taha
Megha Adya
Melissa Walek
Misbah Husain
Mohamadou Mbaye
Muda Yang
Nadia Shaiq & Family
Najma Zamani & Syed
Noorul Huda
Navid Chowdhury
Nicole Ford McCarn
Nikhil Arun
Nora Akila
Nupur Bhardwaj
Olga Bulka
Olivia Tesher
Omar Jeelani
Parisa Siddiqui
Patrick O'Reilly
Patrick Popelka
Pawel Armatys
Peter Panos
Prashanti Kodali
Ravi Shah
Riazuddin Mohammed

Richard Jové
Riley Moore
Roshan Shankar
Sabah Hussain
Saloni Patel
Samantha Gilbert
Sana Khan
Sanaa S. Khan & Family
Sara Ali & Family
Sarah Al-Mayahi
Sarah Felvey
Sean McGowan
Seema K. Khan & Family
Serena Upadhyay
Shamsul Huda
Sharan Arkalgud
Shaun Ali
Sherif ElMasry
Spencer Poklop
Stefan Rebic

Stella Lee
Sydney Mann
Syed B.H. Bokhari & Family
Syed J. Bukhari
Syed Kausar
Tahir Bokhari & Family
Tara Rahman
Tariq Bokhari & Family
Tingliang Huang
Tova R. Margolis
Uma Krishnan
Victor Li
Vijaya Anandan
Vishnu Varada
Wayllon Lu
Yahya Soliman
Zach Rahman
Zaheer Coovadia
Zoey Zheng

APPENDIX

—

INTRODUCTION

Feinberg, Andrew, Madhav Mullapudi, Michael Benore, and Oliver Page. "The Restaurant of the Future." Deloitte, Deloitte Development LLC., 2016. https://www2.deloitte.com/content/dam/Deloitte/us/Documents/consumer-business/us-consumer-business-restaurant-of-the-future-perspective-final.pdf.

Labine-Romain, Adele, Dan Terrill, Jess Mizrahi, Xanthe Smith, and Rhiannon Yetsenga. "The Future of Food." Deloitte, Deloitte Touche Tohmatsu, 2019. https://www2.deloitte.com/content/dam/Deloitte/au/Documents/Economics/deloitte-au-economics-future-food-uber-eats-100719.pdf.

National Restaurant Association. "National Statistics." Accessed June 1, 2020. https://restaurant.org/research/restaurant-statistics/restaurant-industry-facts-at-a-glance.

Obermeier, Kylie. "Nightlife: Yume Wo Katare." BU Today, Boston University, February 11, 2016. http://www.bu.edu/articles/2016/yume-wo-katare-porter-square/.

Parsa, H.G., John T. Self, David Njite, and Tiffany King. "Why Restaurants Fail." Cornell Hotel and Restaurant Administration Quarterly 46, no. 3 (August 2005). https://daniels.du.edu/assets/research-hg-parsa-part-1-2015.pdf.

Ro, Herrine and Luke Hansen. "Why people wait for hours to eat at this tiny Boston ramen workshop." Insider, Insider Inc., September 11, 2019. https://www.insider.com/yume-wo-kotare-boston-ramen-dream-workshop-09-2019.

Roth-Dishy, Amelia F.. "Community Ramen Hotspot Still the Stuff of Dreams." The Harvard Crimson, October 30, 2018. https://www.thecrimson.com/article/2018/10/30/yume-wo-katare-review/.

Shea, Andrea. "Porter Square Ramen Shop Wants To Make Your Dreams Come True." WBUR, WBUR, July 16, 2014. https://www.wbur.org/news/2014/07/16/yume-wo-katare-cambridge-ramen.

Sloan, A. Elizabeth. "It's Time for Restaurant Realignment." Food Technology Magazine 72, no. 10 (October 2018). https://www.ift.org/news-and-publications/food-technology-magazine/issues/2018/october/features/trends-in-restaurant-foodservice.

CHAPTER 1: BACKGROUND

Harford, Tim. "How McDonald's revolutionised business." BBC, February 5, 2020. https://www.bbc.com/news/business-51208592.

Mealy, Lorri. "A History of the Restaurant." The Balance Small Business, Dotdash, December 13, 2018. https://www.thebalancesmb.com/a-history-of-the-restaurant-2888319.

Meares, Hadley. "The Real McDonald's: The San Bernardino Origins of a Fast Food Empire." KCET, Public Media Group of Southern California, August 5, 2016. https://www.kcet.org/food-living/the-real-mcdonalds-the-san-bernardino-origins-of-a-fast-food-empire.

Thompson, Derek. "The Paradox of American Restaurants." The Atlantic, June 20, 2017. https://www.theatlantic.com/business/archive/2017/06/its-the-golden-age-of-restaurants-in-america/530955/.

U.S. Department of Agriculture, Economic Research Service, America's Eating Habits: Food Away From Home, by Michelle J. Saksena, Abigail M. Okrent, Tobenna D. Anekwe, Clare Cho, Christopher Dicken, Anne Effland, Howard Elitzak, Joanne Guthrie, Karen S. Hamrick, Jeffrey Hyman, Young Jo, Biing-Hwan Lin, Lisa Mancino, Patrick W. McLaughlin, Ilya Rahkovsky, Katherine Ralston, Travis A. Smith, Hayden Stewart, Jessica Todd, and Charlotte Tuttle, (September 2018), https://www.ers.usda.gov/webdocs/publications/90228/eib-196.pdf.

White Castle Management Co.. "Our Story." Accessed June 1, 2020. https://www.whitecastle.com/about-us/our-history.

CHAPTER 2: CURRENT STATUS

"2018 Food and Health Survey." International Food Information Council Foundation, 2018. https://foodinsight.org/wp-content/uploads/2018/05/2018-FHS-Report-FINAL.pdf.

National Restaurant Association. "National Restaurant Association Unveils its Restaurant Industry 2030 Report." Accessed June 1, 2020. https://restaurant.org/restaurant-industry-2030-report.

National Restaurant Association. "National Statistics." Accessed June 1, 2020. https://restaurant.org/research/restaurant-statistics/restaurant-industry-facts-at-a-glance.

Reichheld, Ashley, Jeffrey Samotny, Oliver Page, and Stephanie Perrone Goldstein. "Through guests' eyes." Deloitte, Deloitte Development LLC., 2017. https://www2.deloitte.com/us/en/pages/consumer-business/articles/restaurant-customer-experience-strategy.html.

Spyce, Spyce Food Co.. "Who We Are." Accessed June 1, 2020. https://www.spyce.com/who-we-are-2/.

Spycefoodco. "Spyce - Robotic Restaurant by Four MIT Graduates in Collaboration with Chef Daniel Boulud." May 3, 2018. Video, 2:29.
https://www.youtube.com/watch?time_
continue=122&v=9LqqcDL99UA&feature=emb_logo.

Terrell, Kenneth. "McDonald's and AARP Team Up to Fill Jobs." AARP, April 25, 2019.
https://www.aarp.org/work/job-search/info-2019/mcdonalds-partners-with-aarp.html.

CHAPTER 3: ADAPTING INTELLIGENTLY

Fultz, Paul, Joel Rampoldt, and Dan Shaughnessy. "An Appetite for Change." KPMG, KPMG LLP, 2016.
https://assets.kpmg/content/dam/kpmg/pdf/2016/07/kr-gtl-an-appetite-for-change.pdf.

CHAPTER 4: ONLINE ORDERING

Grubhub. "About Us." Accessed June 1, 2020.
https://about.grubhub.com/about-us/what-is-grubhub/default.aspx.

National Restaurant Association. "2019 Restaurant Industry Factbook." National Restaurant Association. Accessed June 1, 2020.
https://restaurant.org/downloads/pdfs/research/soi/restaurant_industry_fact_
sheet_2019.pdf.

Saxena, Jaya. "Delivery Apps Aren't Getting Any Better." Eater, Vox Media, LLC., May 29, 2019.
https://www.eater.com/2019/5/29/18636255/delivery-apps-hurting-restaurants-
grubhub-seamless-ubereats.

Singh, Sarwant. "The Soon To Be $200B Online Food Delivery Is Rapidly Changing The Global Food Industry." Forbes, Forbes Media LLC., September 9, 2019.
https://www.forbes.com/sites/sarwantsingh/2019/09/09/the-soon-to-be-200b-
online-food-delivery-is-rapidly-changing-the-global-food-industry/#78a4eda4b1bc.

UBS Investment Bank, UBS Securities. "Is the Kitchen Dead?" June 18, 2018.
https://www.ubs.com/global/en/investment-bank/in-focus/2018/dead-kitchen.html.

US Foods, US Foods Inc.. "New Study Shows What Consumers Crave in a Food Delivery Service." 2019.
https://www.usfoods.com/our-services/business-trends/2019-food-delivery-
statistics.html.

CHAPTER 5: IN-HOUSE

"Top 10 Benefits of a POS System." Dallas POS, February 15, 2020.
https://www.dallaspossystems.com/tips/top-10-benefits-of-a-pos-system/.

Alicia Kelso, "Self-Order Kiosks Are Finally Having A Moment In The Fast Food Space," Forbes, Forbes Media LLC., July 20, 2019.
https://www.forbes.com/sites/aliciakelso/2019/07/30/self-order-kiosks-are-finally-
having-a-moment-in-the-fast-food-space/#36d16b944275.

Berthiaume, Dan. "Chick-Fil-A eliminates lines with new mobile service." Chain Store Age, EnsembleIQ, October 17, 2019.
https://chainstoreage.com/chick-fil-eliminates-lines-new-mobile-service.

Coskun, Vedat, Busra Ozdenizci, and Kerem Ok. "The Survey on Near Field Communication." Sensors. June 5, 2015.
https://www.ncbi.nlm.nih.gov/pmc/articles/PMC4507650/.

Feemster, Jason. "What is POS? The Definitive Definition and Guide." POS USA, May 21, 2020.
https://www.posusa.com/what-is-pos/.

Feinberg, Andrew, Madhav Mullapudi, Michael Benore, and Oliver Page. "The Restaurant of the Future." Deloitte, Deloitte Development LLC., 2016.
https://www2.deloitte.com/content/dam/Deloitte/us/Documents/consumer-business/us-consumer-business-restaurant-of-the-future-perspective-final.pdf.

Haddon, Heather. "McDonald's Tests Robot Fryers and Voice-Activated Drive-Throughs." The Wall Street Journal, June 20, 2019.
https://www.wsj.com/articles/mcdonalds-tests-robot-fryers-and-voice-activated-drive-throughs-11561060920?mod=searchresults&page=1&pos=1.

Hill, Simon. "What is NCF? Here's everything you need to know." Digital Trends, Designtechnica Corporation, May 6, 2020.
https://www.digitaltrends.com/mobile/what-is-nfc/.

Ingenico Group. "Self-Service Kiosks Are Becoming More Popular in Restaurants." EVO, EVO Payments Inc., August 29, 2019.
https://www.evopayments.us/self-service-kiosks-are-becoming-popular-in-restaurants-heres-why/.

Kaitlin Keefer, "5 Tech Solutions You Need to Grow Your Restaurant Business," SquareUp, Square, Inc.. Accessed June 1, 2020.
https://squareup.com/us/en/townsquare/tech-solutions-for-restaurants.

Luna, Nancy. "Chipotle Mexican Grill quietly rolls out voice AI to 1,800 units." Nation's Restaurant News, Informa USA, Inc., July 20, 2019.
https://www.nrn.com/fast-casual/chipotle-mexican-grill-quietly-rolls-out-voice-ai-1800-units.

Maze, Jonathan. "Chick-Fil-A Introduces Mobile Dine-In Ordering." Restaurant Business Online, Winsight LLC., October 17, 2019.
https://www.restaurantbusinessonline.com/technology/chick-fil-introduces-mobile-dine-ordering.

Rasmussen, Bruce. "8 reasons restaurants need a kiosk strategy." Fast Casual, Networld Media Group, LLC., July 12, 2018.
https://www.fastcasual.com/blogs/8-reasons-restaurants-need-a-kiosk-strategy/.

Romeo, Peter. "Restaurants Admit Strong Fears About Keeping up with Tech." Restaurant Business Online, Winsight LLC., April 23, 2019.
https://www.restaurantbusinessonline.com/technology/restaurants-admit-strong-fears-about-keeping-tech.

Rosenheim, Brita. "The Future of Restaurant Tech: Serving the Next Course."
Forbes, Forbes Media LLC., November 11, 2019.
https://www.forbes.com/sites/themixingbowl/2019/11/11/the-future-of-restaurant-
tech-serving-the-next-course/#33d4d32416dd.

Saltzman, Melanie, Christopher Livesay, Joan Martelli, and Deborah Gouffran, "Is
Fance's groundbreaking food-waste law working?" PBS, NewsHour Productions
LLC., August 21, 2019.
https://www.pbs.org/newshour/show/is-frances-groundbreaking-food-waste-law-working.

CHAPTER 6: AUTOMATION

Chui, Michael, James Manyika, and Mehdi Miremadi, "Where machines could
replace humans—and where they can't (yet)." McKinsey Digital, McKinsey &
Company, July 8, 2016.
https://www.mckinsey.com/business-functions/mckinsey-digital/our-insights/
where-machines-could-replace-humans-and-where-they-cant-yet.

Food Management, Informa USA, Inc.. "Foodservice automation drives ROI."
March 22, 2019.
https://www.food-management.com/build-better-operation/foodservice-
automation-drives-roi.

Hardy, Kevin. "The Digital Revolution." QSR, Journalistic, Inc., November 2014.
https://www.qsrmagazine.com/ordering/digital-revolution.

Holt, Steve. "Full service: Automation in restaurants is changing the food industry."
GreenBiz, GreenBiz Group Inc., June 15, 2018.
https://www.greenbiz.com/article/full-service-automation-restaurants-changing-
food-industry.

Joshi, Naveen. "Bon Appétit! Robotic Restaurants Are The Future." Forbes, Forbes
Media LLC., February 3, 2020.
https://www.forbes.com/sites/cognitiveworld/2020/02/03/bon-apptit-robotic-
restaurants-are-the-future/#14f9afad2136.

Lalley, Heather. "Robot-Powered Spyce Restaurant to Close Temporarily for
Revamp." Restaurant Business Online, Winsight LLC., November 15, 2019.
https://www.restaurantbusinessonline.com/technology/robot-powered-spyce-
restaurant-close-temporarily-revamp.

National Restaurant Association. "National Restaurant Association Unveils its
Restaurant Industry 2030 Report." Accessed June 1, 2020.
https://restaurant.org/restaurant-industry-2030-report.

National Restaurant Association. "National Statistics." Accessed June 1, 2020.
https://restaurant.org/research/restaurant-statistics/restaurant-industry-facts-at-a-glance.

Parsons, Russ. "Artisan rhetoric: Patric Kuh on the growth, definition, and future of
'artisanal' food." The Splendid Table, Minnesota Public Radio, October 11, 2016.
https://www.splendidtable.org/story/artisan-rhetoric-patric-kuh-on-the-growth-
definition-and-future-of-artisanal-food.

Spycefoodco. "Spyce - Robotic Restaurant by Four MIT Graduates in Collaboration with Chef Daniel Boulud." May 3, 2018. Video, 2:29.
https://www.youtube.com/watch?time_
continue=122&v=9LqqcDL99UA&feature=emb_logo.

Tracey Lien, "Olive Garden rolls out tabletop tablets for ordering and payment," Los Angeles Times, April 14, 2015.
https://www.latimes.com/business/technology/la-fi-tn-olive-garden-tablets-20150414-story.html.

CHAPTER 7: BREAKDOWN

Ahmad Kareh. "Evolution of The Four Ps: Revisiting The Marketing Mix." Forbes, Forbes Media LLC., January 3, 2018.
https://www.forbes.com/sites/forbesagencycouncil/2018/01/03/evolution-of-the-four-ps-revisiting-the-marketing-mix/#6da683d41120.

Oyster Sunday, Oyster Sunday LLC.. "About." Accessed June 1, 2020.
https://www.oystersunday.com/about.

Oyster Sunday, Oyster Sunday LLC.. "Reimagining the hospitality industry's business infrastructure." Accessed June 1, 2020.
https://www.oystersunday.com.

Stanford University. "Marketing Strategy." Accessed June 1, 2020.
https://web.stanford.edu/class/ee353/marketing percent2ostrategy.htm.

CHAPTER 8: SOCIAL MEDIA

 "Insights to Go," Facebook for Business, accessed June 1, 2020.
https://www.facebook.com/iq/insights-to-go/6m-there-are-more-than-6-million-active-advertisers-on-facebook.

Barnhart, Brent. "The most important social media trends to know for 2020," SproutSocial, Sprout Social, Inc., May 6, 2020.
https://sproutsocial.com/insights/social-media-trends/.

BrainyQuote. "Gary Vaynerchuk Quotes." Accessed June 1, 2020.
https://www.brainyquote.com/quotes/gary_vaynerchuk_503110.

Gary Vaynerchuk, Gary Vee IP, LLC.. "Gary Vaynerchuk." Accessed June 1, 2020.
https://www.garyvaynerchuk.com/biography/.

GaryVee TV. "How to Market a Restaurant on Social Media." January 16, 2019. Video, 18:25.
https://www.youtube.com/watch?v=TWvaDVmoB5U.

Gourmet Marketing. "Restaurant Social Media Marketing Trends." Accessed June 1, 2020.
https://www.gourmetmarketing.net/restaurant-essentials/social-media-marketing-trends/.

Henderson, Gary. "How Much Do Facebook Ads Cost?" Digital Marketing Blog, DigitalMarketing.org, September 21, 2018.
https://www.digitalmarketing.org/blog/how-much-do-facebook-ads-cost.

Jon Taffer, Jon Taffer, LLC.. "About Jon Taffer." Accessed June 1, 2020.
https://jontaffer.com/about/.

WebFX. "How Restaurants Can Effectively Use Social Media Marketing." Accessed June 1, 2020.
https://www.webfx.com/industries/food-beverage/restaurants/social-media/.

CHAPTER 9: LOYALTY PROGRAMS

Beebe, Julia. "Whip Your Restaurant Loyalty Program Into Shape [Infographic]." Toast, Toast, Inc., February 13, 2018.
https://pos.toasttab.com/blog/restaurant-loyalty-program-infographic.

Bryan, Jordan. "What's Your Customer Effort Score?" Gartner, Gartner, Inc., February 11, 2020.
https://www.gartner.com/smarterwithgartner/unveiling-the-new-and-improved-customer-effort-score/.

Burnett, Sallie. "Restaurants Serve Up Loyalty Programs to Combat Competition." Forbes, Forbes Media LLC., March 25, 2019.
https://www.forbes.com/sites/forbesagencycouncil/2019/03/25/restaurants-serve-up-loyalty-programs-to-combat-competition/#61af25416a94.

Chipotle Mexican Grill. "Chipotle Rewards." Accessed June 1, 2020.
https://www.chipotle.com/order/rewards.

Collins, Emily. "How Consumers Really Feel About Loyalty Programs." Forrester, Forrester Research, Inc., May 8, 2017.
http://www.oracle.com/us/solutions/consumers-loyalty-programs-3738548.pdf.

Crane, Kristin. "How Restaurants Are Using Loyalty Programs to Boost Business." Upserve, Upserve, Inc., July 20, 2018.
https://upserve.com/restaurant-insider/best-restaurant-loyalty-programs-common/.

Frankenfield, Jake. "Churn Rate." Investopedia, Dotdash, May 25, 2020.
https://www.investopedia.com/terms/c/churnrate.asp.

Granat, Jim. "The Pros and Cons of Instituting a Customer Loyalty Program." Forbes, Forbes Media LLC., September 3, 2020.
https://www.forbes.com/sites/forbesfinancecouncil/2019/09/03/the-pros-and-cons-of-instituting-a-customer-loyalty-program/#539fde073f09.

Guild, Adam. "How to Use Your Retargeting to Grow Your Restaurant Revenue." Forbes, Forbes Media LLC., July 16, 2019.
https://www.forbes.com/sites/forbesagencycouncil/2019/07/16/how-to-use-retargeting-to-grow-your-restaurant-revenue/#559e2fd67b23.

Medallia. "Net Promoter Score." Accessed June 1, 2020.
https://www.medallia.com/net-promoter-score/.

Papageorgiou, Kostas. "5 Must Have Customer Retention Metrics." Userlike, August 31, 2016.
https://www.userlike.com/en/blog/customer-retention-metrics.

Ponomarov, Slava. "Great Restaurant Loyalty Apps and How to Build One." QSR Magazine, Journalistic, Inc., September 2019.
https://www.qsrmagazine.com/outside-insights/great-restaurant-loyalty-apps-and-how-build-one.

Qualtrics. "What is Customer Effort Score (CES) & How Do I Measure It?" Accessed June 1, 2020.
https://www.qualtrics.com/experience-management/customer/customer-effort-score/.

Reichheld, Frederick F. and Phil Schefter. "The Economics of E-Loyalty." Harvard Business School, President & Fellows of Harvard College, June 7, 2000.
https://hbswk.hbs.edu/archive/the-economics-of-e-loyalty.

Shopify. "Upselling." Accessed June 1, 2020.
https://www.shopify.com/encyclopedia/upselling.

Starbucks Coffee Company. "Starbucks Rewards." Accessed June 1, 2020.
https://www.starbucks.com/rewards/.

Starbucks Stories and News, Starbucks Corporation. "Starbucks to enhance industry-leading Starbucks Rewards loyalty program." March 19, 2019.
https://stories.starbucks.com/press/2019/starbucks-to-enhance-industry-leading-starbucks-rewards-loyalty-program/.

Tim. "What is Customer Effort Score (CES) & How to Measure It?" Customer Success (Blog), Retently, December 6, 2018.
https://www.retently.com/blog/customer-effort-score/.

Virgillito, Dan. "How to Calculate Customer Retention Rate (and Improve Yours)." Cooper Chronicles (Blog), Cooper CRM, Inc., September 27, 2018.
https://www.copper.com/blog/customer-retention-rate.

WebstaurantStore, WebsaurantStore Food Service Equipment and Supply Company. "Restaurant Loyalty Programs." April 26, 2019.
https://www.webstaurantstore.com/article/125/starting-loyalty-rewards-programs.html.

Wertz, Jia. "Don't Spend 5 Times More Attracting New Customers, Nurture The Existing Ones." Forbes, Forbes Media LLC., September 12, 2018.
https://www.forbes.com/sites/jiawertz/2018/09/12/dont-spend-5-times-more-attracting-new-customers-nurture-the-existing-ones/#1c8c3f595a8e.

CHAPTER 10: DIGITAL STRATEGY

Dobrila, Andreea. "Growing Restaurant Trends in 2019, According to Industry Experts." GloriaFood, Global Food Tech SRL., January 28, 2019.
https://www.gloriafood.com/restaurant-trends-in-2019.

Everett, Holly. "Digital Marketing for Restaurants: How to Get Found Online." Upserve, Upserve, Inc., January 31, 2019.

Muller, Britney. "SEO 101." Moz, Moz Inc.. Accessed June 1, 2020.
https://moz.com/beginners-guide-to-seo/why-search-engine-marketing-is-necessary.

Sacred Heart University. "The Importance of a Digital Marketing Strategy in Today's World." Accessed June 1, 2020.
https://www.sacredheart.edu/academics/colleges--schools/college-of-business--technology/departments/marketing/digital-marketing-blog/the-importance-of-a-digital-marketing-strategy-in-todays-world/.

CHAPTER 11: FOOD WASTE

FoodPrint, GRACE Communications Foundation. "The Problem of Food Waste."
Accessed June 1, 2020.
https://foodprint.org/issues/the-problem-of-food-waste/.

Gunders, Dana, Jonathan Bloom, JoAnne Berkenkamp, Darby Hoover, Andrea
Spacht, and Marie Mourad. "Wasted: How America is losing up to 40 Percent of its
food from farm to fork." Natural Resources Defense Council, August 2017.
https://www.nrdc.org/sites/default/files/wasted-2017-report.pdf.

Restaurant Business, Restaurant Business Online, Winsight LLC.. "Bowl over
consumers with eco-friendly packaging." October 21, 2019.
https://www.restaurantbusinessonline.com/topics/bowl-over-consumers-eco-
friendly-packaging.

Schwaner-Albright, Oliver. "Five-Star Dining on Leftover Scraps?" The Wall Street
Journal, June 22, 2015.
https://www.wsj.com/articles/zero-waste-restaurants-five-star-dining-on-leftover-
scraps-1434386371.

Starbucks Stories and News, Starbucks Corporation. "Black Friday and Cyber
Monday: New gifts and deals coming to Starbucks." November 19, 2019.
https://stories.starbucks.com/press/2019/black-friday-and-cyber-monday-new-gifts-
and-deals-coming-to-starbucks/.

Taylor, Anne. "Restaurants struggle with food donation laws." The Daily Universe,
November 27, 2017.
https://universe.byu.edu/2017/11/27/confusion-abounds-over-how-to-make-food-
donations-in-utah-1/.

WebstaurantStore, WebsaurantStore Food Service Equipment and Supply Company.
"Ways to Reduce Food Waste in Your Restaurant." August 6, 2018.
https://www.webstaurantstore.com/article/140/how-to-reduce-waste-in-restaurants.html.

CHAPTER 12: LOCAL SOURCING

Angelo White, Dana. "Is it Worth it to Join a CSA?" Food Network, Television Food
Network, April 2009.
https://www.foodnetwork.com/healthyeats/2009/04/joining-a-csa.

Chartered Institute of Procurement & Supply. "The Pros and Cons of Local
Sourcing." Accessed June 1, 2020.
https://www.cips.org/knowledge/procurement-topics-and-skills/srm-and-sc-
management/global-supply-chains/the-pros-and-cons-of-local-sourcing/.

Dunning, Rebecca. "Research-Based Support and Extension Outreach for Local
Food Systems." Center for Environmental Farming Systems, November 2011.
https://cefs.ncsu.edu/wp-content/uploads/research-based-support-for-local-food-
systems.pdf.

Grand Central Bakery. "About." Accessed June 1, 2020.
https://www.grandcentralbakery.com/menus/.

Grand Central Bakery. "Menus." Accessed June 1, 2020.
https://www.grandcentralbakery.com/menus/.

Janzer, Cinnamon, "The History of the Farm to Table Movement." Upserve, Upserve,
Inc., June 22, 2018.
https://upserve.com/restaurant-insider/history-farm-table-movement/.

Mealy, Lorri. "Local Food trends for Restaurants." The Balance Small Business,
January 18, 2020.
https://www.thebalancesmb.com/local-food-trends-for-restaurants-2888604.

National Restaurant Association. "The State of Restaurant Sustainability 2018."
National Restaurant Association. Accessed June 1, 2020.
https://restaurant.org/downloads/pdfs/sustainability/restaurant_sustainability_
research_report_2018.pdf.

National Restaurant Association. "What's Hot: 2019 Culinary Forecast." Accessed
June 1, 2020.
https://www.restaurant.org/downloads/pdfs/research/whatshot/whatshotfinal2019).

Reynolds, Jennifer. "What Is Behind The Trend Of Local Food?" Food Secure
Canada, Winter 2016.
https://foodsecurecanada.org/resources-news/news-media/buying-local-food-products.

San Diego Farmer Bureau. "Sourcing Locally for Restaurants." Accessed June 1, 2020.
https://www.sdfarmbureau.org/wp-content/uploads/2017/09/Sourcing-Locally-for-
Restaurants-8.6.14.pdf.

Torres, Nicole. "Why Sourcing Local Food Is So Hard for Restaurants." Harvard
Business Review, June 15, 2016.
https://hbr.org/2016/06/why-sourcing-local-food-is-so-hard-for-restaurants.

U.S. Department of Agriculture. "Seasonal Produce Guide." Accessed June 1, 2020.
https://snaped.fns.usda.gov/seasonal-produce-guide.

Uncommon Ground. "Organic Rooftop Farm." Accessed June 1, 2020.
https://www.uncommonground.com/roof-top-farm.

CHAPTER 13: CREATING SHARED VALUE

Porter, Michael E., and Mark R. Kramer. "Creating Shared Value." Harvard Business
Review, August 25, 2015.
https://hbr.org/2011/01/the-big-idea-creating-shared-value.

"Watch CNBC's full interview with Shake Shack's CEO Randy Garutti." CNBC,
June 21, 2019. Video, 8:07.
https://www.cnbc.com/video/2019/06/21/watch-cnbcs-full-interview-with-shake-
shacks-ceo-randy-garutti.html.

Farkas, David. "Fine Dining Takes On Fast Casual." US Foods, US Foods Inc..
Accessed June 1, 2020.
https://www.usfoods.com/great-food/food-trends/fine-dining-takes-on-fast-casual.html.

Shake Shack. "Grill & Chill this Summer with Recipes for our Flat-Top Dogs, Revealed in 'Shake Shack: Recipes & Stories.'" April 28, 2017. https://www.shakeshack.com/2017/04/28/grill-chill-summer-recipes-flat-top-dogs-revealed-shake-shack-recipes-stories/.

TEDx Talks. "The Convergence of Casual and Fine | Danny Meyer | TEDx Manhattan." March 20, 2015. Video, 17:36. TEDx Manhattan: https://www.youtube.com/watch?v=5HVdOExw8Dw.

Tidwell, Brandon. "Creating Shared Value." Darden Digest (Blog), Darden Concepts, Inc., October 10, 2013. https://www.darden.com/blog/creating-shared-value.

U.S. Securities and Exchange Commission. "Form 10-K." Accessed June 1, 2020. https://www.investor.gov/introduction-investing/investing-basics/glossary/form-10-k.

Union Square Hospitality Group. "Danny Meyer." Accessed June 1, 2020. https://www.ushgnyc.com/team_member/danny-meyer/.

United States Securities and Exchange Commission, Form 10-K Shake Shack Inc. (2018). https://www.sec.gov/Archives/edgar/data/1620533/000162053319000010/shak-20181226_10k.htm.

Wiener-Bronner, Danielle. "Inside Shake Shack's unusual global strategy." CNN, June 18, 2019. https://www.cnn.com/2019/06/18/business/shake-shack-mexico-city/index.html.

CHAPTER 14: MENU OPTIONS

"IFT18: Generation Z Set To Impact The Future Of Food And Drink Innovation." Mintel, Mintel Group Ltd, July 16, 2018. https://www.mintel.com/press-centre/food-and-drink/generation-z-set-to-impact-the-future-of-food-and-drink-innovation.

Amin, Hiba. "10 Trends Shaping the Restaurant Industry in 2019." ChefHero, March 21, 2019. https://www.chefhero.com/blog/trends-shaping-the-restaurant-industry-in-2019.

Egan, Beth. "Chapter 4 - Menus." Introduction to Food Production and Service. PennState, Accessed June 1, 2020. https://psu.pb.unizin.org/hmd329/chapter/ch4/.

Ferdman, Roberto. "Americans are tired of long restaurant menus." The Washington Post, September 18, 2014. https://www.washingtonpost.com/news/wonk/wp/2014/09/18/americans-are-tired-of-long-restaurant-menus/.

Forgrieve, Janet. "U.S. Restaurant Chains Make Plant-Based Options To Fit Their Brands." Forbes, Forbes Media LLC., February 29, 2020. https://www.forbes.com/sites/janetforgrieve/2020/02/29/us-restaurant-chains-make-plant-based-options-to-fit-their-brands/#3af4ec3c7716.

Gray, Richard. "The secret tricks hidden inside restaurant menus." BBC, November 20, 2017. https://www.bbc.com/future/article/20171120-the-secret-tricks-hidden-inside-restaurant-menus.

HappyCow Healthy Eating Guide. "Vegan & Vegetarian Restaurants in USA."
Accessed June 1, 2020.
https://www.happycow.net/north_america/usa/?filters=vegan-vegetarian-
vegfriendly-chains.

Kateman, Brian. "Vegan Restaurants Are On The Rise." Forbes, Forbes Media LLC.,
August 21, 2019.
https://www.forbes.com/sites/briankateman/2019/08/21/vegan-restaurants-are-on-
the-rise/#7f624541e80f.

Kelso, Alicia Kelso. "The Foods You'll Be Ordering In 2020, According To
Postmates, Grubhub, Uber Eats And DoorDash." Forbes, Forbes Media LLC.,
December 10, 2019.
https://www.forbes.com/sites/aliciakelso/2019/12/10/delivery-companies-predict-
food-trends-for-2020-based-on-customers-ordering-habits/#6c2835c29165.

Liem Beckett, Emma. "6 restaurant trends that could turn tables in 2019."
Restaurant Dive, Industry Dive, January 7, 2019.
https://www.restaurantdive.com/news/6-restaurant-trends-that-could-turn-
tables-in-2019-1/545323/.

Lister, Jonathan. "What is Dissonance in Marketing?" Chron, Hearst Newspapers,
LLC. Accessed June 1, 2020.
https://smallbusiness.chron.com/dissonance-marketing-25900.html.

Littman, Julie and Emma Liem Beckett. "5 restaurant trends that will define 2020."
Restaurant Dive, Industry Dive, Accessed June 1, 2020.
https://www.restaurantdive.com/news/5-restaurant-trends-that-will-
define-2020/569780/.

Mintel, Mintel Group Ltd. "Taste Is The Top Reason Us Consumers Eat Plant-based
Proteins." February 15, 2018.
https://www.mintel.com/press-centre/food-and-drink/taste-is-the-top-reason-us-
consumers-eat-plant-based-proteins.

Postmates. "A Year in Postmates: What We Ordered 2019." Medium, December 9, 2019.
https://blog.postmates.com/a-year-in-postmates-what-we-ordered-2019-
b947cfbfa771.

Souley Vegan. "Press." Accessed June 1, 2020.
https://souleyvegan.com/press.

CHAPTER 15: EXPERIMENTING

Turnwald, Bradley, Danielle Boles, and Alia Crum. "Association Between Indulgent
Descriptions and Vegetable Consumption: Twisted Carrots and Dynamite Beets."
JAMA Internal Medicine 177, no. 8 (August 2017).
https://mbl.stanford.edu/sites/g/files/sbiybj9941/f/turnwaldbolescrum_
indulgentdescriptionsandvegetableconsumption.pdf.

"IFT18: Generation Z Set To Impact The Future Of Food And Drink Innovation."
Mintel, Mintel Group Ltd, July 16, 2018.
https://www.mintel.com/press-centre/food-and-drink/generation-z-set-to-impact-
the-future-of-food-and-drink-innovation.

Andrews, Ryan. "Menu Engineering: How to Increase Profits by 20 percent (Step-by-Step Guide)." Eat, April 15, 2019.
https://restaurant.eatapp.co/blog/food-cost/menu-engineering.

Filloon, Whitney. "Why Restaurants are So Hungry for Your Personal Data." Eater, Vox Media, LLC., October 10, 2018.
https://www.eater.com/2018/10/10/17957350/restaurants-data-mining-personal-information-privacy-loyalty-programs.

Fossett, Jeff, Duncan Gilchrist, and Michael Luca. "Using Experiments to Launch New Products." Harvard Business Review, November 5, 2018.
https://hbr.org/2018/11/using-experiments-to-launch-new-products.

Hensel, Kelly. "2020 Flavor Forecast." Food Technology Magazine 73, no. 12 (December 1, 2019).
https://www.ift.org/news-and-publications/food-technology-magazine/issues/2019/december/features/2020-flavor-forecast.

Luna, Nancy. "MenuMasters 2019: Best New Item." Nation's Restaurant News, Informa USA, Inc., March 27, 2019.
https://www.nrn.com/quick-service/menumasters-2019-best-new-item.

Luna, Nancy. "Taco Bell's global chief food innovation officer Liz Matthews develops inventive menu items." Nation's Restaurant News, Informa USA, Inc., January 22, 2020.
https://www.nrn.com/people/taco-bell-s-global-chief-food-innovation-officer-liz-matthews-develops-inventive-menu-items.

RestoHub, Touch Bistro Inc.. "Restaurant Menu Engineering: Increasing Profits." Accessed June 1, 2020.
https://www.restohub.org/operations/menu/restaurant-menu-engineering/.

Van Duyne, Allie, "How to Make Your Menu a Money-Maker." Toast, Toast, Inc.. Accessed June 1, 2020.
https://pos.toasttab.com/blog/on-the-line/menu-engineering-menu-design.

CHAPTER 16: SEASONALITY

Cooper, Mark. "Food for Thought: Trends in Menu Design." IIAC, January 16, 2018.
http://www.iacconline.org/iacc-blog/food-for-thought-trends-in-menu-design.

Costa, Kristen. "Why Your Restaurant Should Embrace Seasonal Menus." Upserve, Upserve, Inc., February 9, 2018.
https://upserve.com/restaurant-insider/why-your-restaurant-should-embrace-seasonal-menus/.

Homegrown Stories. "Sourcing Food Locally." Accessed June 1, 2020.
https://www.homegrownstories.org/nate-whitley-sourcing-food-locally.

Menus of Change, The Culinary Institute of America. "Principles of Healthy, Sustainable Menus." Accessed June 1, 2020.
https://www.menusofchange.org/principles-resources/moc-principles/.

Mintel, Mintel Group Ltd. "Seasonal Dining Trends - US - June 2019." July 16, 2018.
https://www.mintel.com/press-centre/food-and-drink/generation-z-set-to-impact-the-future-of-food-and-drink-innovation.

Nature's Path, Nature's Path Foods. "What's in Season All Year Round [Seasonal Produce Guide]." September 29, 2016.
https://www.naturespath.com/en-us/blog/whats-in-season-all-year-round-seasonal-produce-guide/.

CHAPTER 17: SERVICE/INTERACTION

American Express, American Express Company. "U.S. Consumers – Especially Millennials – Say Businesses Are Meeting Or Exceeding Their Service Expectations." December 15, 2017.
https://about.americanexpress.com/press-release/wellactually-americans-say-customer-service-better-ever.

Stephens, Regans. "These Will Be the Biggest Food Trends of 2020, According to Chefs." Food & Wine, Meredith Corporation, December 11, 2019.
https://www.foodandwine.com/travel/restaurants/biggest-food-trends-chefs-2020.

Wally's Place Bagel & Deli. "Home." Accessed June 1, 2020.
http://www.wallysplacevt.com/.

CHAPTER 18: WAIT TIME

Egan, Colleen. "How to Reduce Wait Time at Your Restaurant." Square, Square Inc., Accessed June 1, 2020.
https://squareup.com/us/en/townsquare/reduce-restaurant-wait-time.

Palawatta, T.M.B. "Waiting Times and Defining Customer Satisfaction." Vidyodaya Journal of Management 1, no. 1 (June 2015).
https://pdfs.semanticscholar.org/fe5a/15b4934b35cb9d7319538ce4f0fd141838bb.pdf.

Singh, Lisa. "What's On Your Plate? OpenTable Reveals Dining Trends for 2019." OpenTable, OpenTable Inc., December 2, 2019.
https://press.opentable.com/news-releases/news-release-details/whats-your-plate-opentable-reveals-dining-trends-2019.

Toast, Toast, Inc.. "Spoken Cafe Busts the Morning Rush with Toast." Accessed June 1, 2020.
https://pos.toasttab.com/customers/spoken-cafe.

CHAPTER 19: DESIGN

Brew Lab Coffee, "Experience." Accessed June 1, 2020.
https://www.brewlab.coffee/experience.

Green Dining Alliance. "Avenue Restaurant." Accessed June 1, 2020.
https://greendiningalliance.org/location/avenue-restaurant/.

Le Cordon Bleu, Le Cordon Bleu International B.V.. "The secret psychology behind restaurant design." Accessed June 1, 2020.
https://www.cordonbleu.edu/news/the-secret-psychology-behind-restaurant-design/en.

Liem Beckett, Emma. "6 restaurant trends that could turn tables in 2019."
Restaurant Dive, Industry Dive, January 7, 2019.
https://www.restaurantdive.com/news/6-restaurant-trends-that-could-turn-
tables-in-2019-1/545323/.

Lucas, Amelia. "Restaurants are investing in photogenic decor to attract Instagram
users." CNBC, April 19, 2019.
https://www.cnbc.com/2019/04/19/restaurants-invest-in-photogenic-decor-to-
attract-instagram-users.html.

Pietro NoLita. "Healthy Italian Cuisine," Accessed June 1, 2020.
https://www.pietronolita.com/.

Restaurant Essentials, Gourmet Marketing. "Restaurant Design Trends." Accessed
June 1, 2020.
https://www.gourmetmarketing.net/restaurant-essentials/restaurant-design-trends/.

Schild, Darcy. "10 food and restaurant trends that will define how people eat in
2020." Insider, Insider Inc., November 11, 2019.
https://www.insider.com/food-restaurant-trend-outlook-2020.

CHAPTER 20: UNIQUE SELLING PROPOSITION

Bovino, Arthur and Dan Myers. "The 101 Best Pizzas in America." The Daily Meal,
Tribune Publishing, September 27, 2019.
https://www.thedailymeal.com/101-best-pizzas-america-2019.

Chefmanship Academy, Unilever Food Solutions. "Topic 1: 5 Types of Service."
Accessed June 1, 2020.
https://www.unileverfoodsolutions.com.ph/chef-inspiration/chefmanship-academy/
module-7-service-service-service/topic-1-5-types-of-service.html.

Dig. "We're Making A Difference." Accessed June 1, 2020.
https://www.diginn.com/community-and-csr/.

Falafel Inc. "Fresh Ingredients. Authentic food. Real impact." Accessed June 1, 2020.
https://www.falafelinc.org/#our_story.

Flaherty, Devon. "How Far Can the Grab-and-Go Trend Go?" QSR, Journalistic,
Inc., November 2018.
https://www.qsrmagazine.com/menu-innovations/how-far-can-grab-and-go-trend-go.

Grubhub for Restaurants, "Creating a Unique Selling Proposition For Your
Restaurant." January 3, 2019.
https://get.grubhub.com/blog/create-unique-selling-prop.html.

Krystal, Becky. "This $3 falafel sandwich is one of the best cheap meals in
Washington." The Washington Post, June 16, 2017.
https://www.washingtonpost.com/news/going-out-guide/wp/2017/06/16/this-3-
falafel-sandwich-is-one-of-the-best-cheap-meals-in-washington/.

Liem Beckett, Emma. "6 restaurant trends that could turn tables in 2019."
Restaurant Dive, Industry Dive, January 7, 2019.
https://www.restaurantdive.com/news/6-restaurant-trends-that-could-turn-
tables-in-2019-1/545323/.

Matthew. "The Promotional Power of a Signature Dish." Gourmet Marketing, August 30, 2013. https://www.gourmetmarketing.net/the-promotional-power-of-a-signature-dish/.

Mike's Pastry. "History." Accessed June 1, 2020. https://www.mikespastry.com/history/.

Paradita Eatery. "About Us." Accessed June 1, 2020. http://paradita.com/about-us/.

S'MAC. "Our Story." Accessed June 1, 2020. http://www.eatsmac.com/our-story/.

Schild, Darcy. "10 food and restaurant trends that will define how people eat in 2020." Insider, Insider Inc., November 11, 2019. https://www.insider.com/food-restaurant-trend-outlook-2020.

Taylor, Kate. "Chick-fil-A is taking over America by offering the best customer service in fast food." Business Insider, Insider Inc., June 26, 2019. https://www.businessinsider.com/chick-fil-a-best-customer-service-in-fast-food-2019-6.